CONTENTS

INTRODUCTION

Those who can DO
  Those who can't TEACH
    And those who can't teach...?

The old saw which has delighted each group of pupils or students who discovered it afresh has, in recent years, acquired sadly ironical overtones. Some teachers who want to teach can't — there isn't a teaching job for them. What can they do?

I first wrote those words seven years ago as the opening paragraph of the forerunner of this book. I had written it in response to the seemingly endless stream of final year students worried by the prospect of no teaching job at the end of their course. 'What else can I do?' was the constantly reiterated question.

There were other opening remarks to the interviews. 'I don't know what to do. I want to hang on till I get a teaching post. Can I do something useful in the meanwhile?' 'Should I take any old job now, or wait till I get what I want?' 'What are my chances of getting a job in X — where my fiancé lives?' 'Are there other kinds of teaching job?' 'I'd like to apply for this graduate training scheme but would they consider a BEd?' 'It's all been such a waste. I don't know where to begin.'

I had gone over the same ground so often both in terms of offering factual information and in terms of suggesting the issues that needed to be faced, that I thought a few notes which students could read at leisure, perhaps before or between interviews, would be a good idea. I had masses of careers books but none of them began at the point my students were at. No good saying like the man in the story, 'If I were you I wouldn't start from here!' I needed something that started from the very place they were at. Then I began to consider the value of notes in a format which could be sent through the post to students who had left but were without a job and had written to us when they were, in many cases, at a point of desperation. That was why I wrote essays not notes, and adopted a more personal tone than is perhaps the case in much careers literature.

It was from this duplicated booklet that the first edition of *What Can a Teacher Do Except Teach?* developed. The encouraging reception given to it has led to this completely revised and expanded edition.

In 1975 I had hoped that as the cut-back in teacher training places took effect the job situation for teachers would ease. It has not, and the response to the first edition has demonstrated clearly that such a book is needed by the practising teacher faced with or worried about redundancy, as well as by the newly-qualified. I have therefore given much more space and attention to the question of career change for the experienced teacher. The more detailed discussion of many of the alternative careers and the addition of more specific examples will, I hope, make this edition even more useful to the other groups — viz. sixth formers who are considering teacher training and the many trained women teachers who left the profession to marry, expecting to return when their families were grown-up.

There have always been trained teachers who took up other careers. Perhaps they decided teaching wasn't for them; perhaps they taught for a few years and then moved on quite naturally into other fields. The loss of highly qualified personnel into industry and commerce used to be a standard filler article for the feature pages in the local and national press. It has been superseded by one on the unemployed teacher working shifts in the local factory.

This booklet cannot provide you with a job. It cannot give you, as an individual, directions on what to do. What it does is to give you as much information as we can pack into a small space on how to find out about jobs in teaching and other quite different employment areas. It has been divided into sections so that you can select the one most relevant to your particular needs — and it has indexes so you can see which careers are referred to inside and where to find general topics such as 'the probationary year'.

Selecting a completely new career may involve some difficult decisions on your part. Many industrial, commercial and public organisations do their major recruiting of school and university leavers early in the year, whilst many local authorities will not be appointing to schools until late in the summer term. If you are a final year student, choosing another career may mean making the decision to try something different *now*, i.e. *before* you discover you can't get a teaching job.

No book can make your decision for you, but it can guide you to the information you may need before you decide how to cope with what may be a difficult situation.

Colleagues in other institutions all over the country and careers officers who find teachers among their clients have used the book, and their comments on it and the discussions I have had with many of them on this question have obviously influenced my revisions. In particular, I must mention discussions with my colleagues and friends in the Association of Careers Advisers in Colleges of Higher Education (ACACHE).

Lastly — and most importantly — I must thank the former students who have fed back to my college and to me information about their new careers. What I said about them in 1980 still holds: I must add that in several years of helping students find alternative careers, my overwhelming impression has been of the very best qualities associated with teachers. Their philosophical outlook would have done justice to the noblest of the Greeks. They have not railed at the injustice of their fate, nor have they expressed their intentions to get the taxpayer to keep them when they couldn't find the job they were trained to do. (And in many cases had been *urged* to train for because their talents were so much needed!) Their main fault, in fact, has been too strong a tendency to self-deprecation.

No wonder when they have conquered *that*, that so many of them have been so successful in their new careers.

LOOKING FOR THAT FIRST POST

This section is directed particularly at those who have recently qualified and want a teaching job. It covers a very broad range of work, however, including teaching adults in settings far removed from the conventional classroom, and will therefore also be of interest to experienced teachers seeking a change, or married women hoping to be "returners". It should also be of interest to those, both pupils at school and adults seeking a new career, who are considering teacher training and are concerned about the opportunities.

This section begins with observations on the current employment situation for new teachers, gives general advice on strategies for the job-search (though mature students should also consult Section Six) and then surveys opportunities in teaching. A list of addresses of useful organisations is appended.

The Employment Market and You
There was a time when it was relatively easy for final year students to obtain their first teaching posts; indeed, by writing to several authorities they may have enjoyed the pleasure of choosing the school that appealed most. Then came the savage cuts in posts

as a result of an over-production of teachers for a falling school population. The present economic difficulties of the country have not eased the situation.

The drop in the birth rate, which affected the primary sector so severely four or five years ago, is now having its impact upon secondary posts, so that specialist subject teachers too, particularly if they are offering English combined with drama or history, are experiencing difficulties in getting their first appointment. A substantial number of the newly-qualified are still seeking posts six months after qualifying and around 10 or 11% annually do not obtain teaching jobs in schools at all, but go into quite different employment.

From 1980 onwards there has been an increasing trend towards the 'temporary' post. Any careers adviser in a college with trainee teachers will know of a number of finalists each year who take up 'temporary' teaching appointments — sometimes for a year, sometimes for a term, often for maternity cover. (The Department of Education and Science (DES) statistical survey of first teaching appointments does not, incidentally, distinguish between permanent and temporary posts.) I have known several teachers who completed their probationary year in different schools as 'temps'. Such experience does often lead to a permanent post.

All these different factors combine to create a situation which is fluid and uncertain and worrying for new teachers. Even the number of likely vacancies is difficult for authorities to estimate. When I'm asked by a student, 'Frankly, what do you think the job situation will be like in county X or town Y?' I think the most honest answer is often, 'It will all depend on the births, deaths and relocations!' Redeployment, too, can have its effect, but adversely, on vacancies for new teachers. Incidentally, if you are only at the stage of considering teacher training, don't be mesmerised by the latest figures on 'over-supply' or shortage subjects. By all means take them into your considerations but don't base a decision entirely on them. Remember that a sudden surge in applicants for, say, chemistry or physics courses could have a dramatic effect on those particular 'shortage' subjects, and more importantly, the chances of success of any individual new teacher are affected by so many factors, local and personal, other than national supply and demand. Naturally all this is disappointing especially if relatives a few years older than you waltzed into their first job *and* expected rapid promotion.

I am often asked how many applications for jobs one should expect to have to make. There is no straightforward answer to this. Averages would be of little use because the experience of students is so variable. It is certainly quite common to have to make more than 30 applications, and every year I know of one or two teachers, especially those geographically limited, who have made two or three applications, and from these had a couple of interviews and a job offer. Clearly this level of success reflects circumstances such as knowing the school and selecting jobs for which one has ideal qualifications. Those who make 80 applications have inevitably included jobs for which their chance of success was small. It is likely too that they need to look at their application technique (see Section Eight).

If repeated applications and even interviews seem to be producing no results, it is easy to get depressed. It is important then to remember that you are not alone, and indeed that this is not a new phenomenon. I well recall a speaker at a careers conference, a rather unworldly-looking don who seemed as if the harsh commercial world had never whitened her locks, surprising the audience by remaining unmoved by tales of PhDs writing a dozen letters without a sniff of a job. She had herself once written upwards of

30, she said, had six interviews and two offers. One more than she needed to start a career.

Many of the older people you meet in interesting posts, at one time or another have applied for job after job before they struck lucky. Eventually their persistence was rewarded. If the jobs didn't come looking for them, they went out hunting the jobs. Where do you start today? Traditionally local authorities appointed probationary teachers either to a particular school (commonly in the case of specialist posts) or to the authority 'pool' (commonly in the case of primary posts), from which at a later date specific vacancies were filled. Many local authorities have now discontinued the 'pool' system and advise applicants to respond to advertisements as and when they appear.

Institutions which train teachers should have a member of staff in contact with the local authorities, who can give some information as to the current policy and vacancy position, but it is only realistic to expect that in some cases, until quite late in the spring term — even the summer term, the replies will be on the lines of 'policy under review' and 'vacancy position not known at present'.

Job-Search Strategies
You would be well advised to consult the *Times Educational Supplement* regularly, also *The Guardian* and other national papers as well as such publications as *The Teacher*. As far as Scotland is concerned adverts for vacancies appear from time to time in the Scottish Educational Journal (published by the Educational Institute of Scotland, 46 Moray Place, Edinburgh) in the Times Educational Supplement (Scottish Division) and in the Scottish daily press. It is also open to a teacher to write to an education authority or to the governing body of a school to enquire about opportunities of employment.

Remember that both local authorities and independent schools are cutting their budgets — and that includes advertising. Posts are no longer being advertised in half a dozen different papers. As there is less duplication, it is well worth looking at all the newspapers and periodicals you can. If you have relatives in another part of the country, ask them to keep an eye on local daily and weekly papers and send you cuttings of possible vacancies. Individual schools sometimes advertise only locally because they believe they get a better response for their money. There are cases of advertising being restricted to a single publication.

There is an increasing tendency for local authorities to advertise primary posts, and temporary as well as part-time posts, *only* in local newspapers. This is partly on grounds of cost, but also to limit the number of applications and to attract locally-based teachers. Some authorities give details of their advertising policies to teacher training institutions. A few issue regular vacancy bulletins, which can be sent on receipt of stamped addressed envelopes. Use first class stamps. Second class seems to take so long that the closing dates for applications have gone by the time the vacancy bulletin reaches you. Some posts are notified direct to the local teacher training institutions.

In considering which jobs to apply for you should be as flexible as you realistically can with regard to age-range, geographical situation and the type of school. Although you may have trained as, say, an infant teacher, this does not preclude you from being employed in a secondary school in England and Wales and there have certainly been instances of graduates being employed as secondary mathematics, language or English teachers even though they trained for the five to nine age-group. This does not apply in

Scotland, however, where the relationship between job and training is highly specific. For further information on registration and employment as a teacher in Scotland write to Scottish Education Department, 43 Jeffrey Street, Edinburgh EH1 1DN.

Limited mobility is probably the greatest single cause of teachers failing to obtain teaching posts. If you are in this position, it is vital to be as flexible as you can in other directions. Married women are often financially in a position to take up part-time or short-term temporary posts. These should definitely not be despised. Apart from giving useful work experience, these jobs keep you in touch with the local educational scene. Heads have their unofficial grapevine and it is by no means unknown for the part-timer or 'temp' to be lined up for a full-time post in the same school, or recommended for a local vacancy elsewhere. I know of a case where the headmistress was so impressed by a teacher covering for maternity leave that, when she applied for a post in a prestigious comprehensive, the head telephoned the school to say, 'Snap her up! I only wish I could keep her'. She got the job. Part-time work which is regular (e.g. a half-time post) does count towards the completion of the probationary period. The total period for part-timers is determined on an individual basis.

In considering the independent sector it is worth noting that, although the probationary year may not be undertaken in an independent school, there is *no* specified time limit within which it must be completed. Local authorities have been given some encouragement by the DES to recommend the waiver of some, or even all, of the probationary period in the case of teachers with 'good experience and substantial satisfactory service reliably vouched for' moving from an independent school into a maintained one. The authority has to be satisfied that the period of service was sufficiently long, and also that the conditions of work were sufficiently similar to those in a maintained school, for the authority to be confident that the teacher will be successful in the maintained sector.

One of the things you should certainly do is to think carefully about what you have to offer in terms of talents, academic and practical strengths, experience (e.g. teaching practice, field work in other courses, any relevant temporary work you may have done) and specific relevant interests, as exemplified in your college activities, special options selected in your course and interests outside college life. Start a personal file which should include a detailed dossier of all relevant experience. You will find further advice on this in Section Eight.

It is astonishing how many final year students have never systematically assessed their personal strengths and particular expertise. When selecting advertisements bear these qualities in mind and gear your letters of application to the specific requirements of each post. (Keep a copy of each letter so that if you get an interview you will be able to refresh your memory as to exactly what you told the head!) A judicious selection of strong points can give your application an emphasis highly relevant to a particular job. For example, a course option on remedial English work, involvement in a project on language acquisition or reading schemes, together with an appropriate reference to some work on teaching practice, can present a picture of someone well able to support the remedial scheme in a school. Too many applicants think little further than age-range and main subject in presenting their course experience.

The deciding factor between two similarly qualified candidates is often the 'extra' contribution they can make to the school. For example, I know of a history teacher who was interviewed for a history post because his course options included one on careers education and the head thought it would be a useful extra contribution to the school. He did in fact get the history job, was able to be involved in careers work in the school, and indeed subsequently switched his energies and interests to careers education. I have known more than one junior teacher get an interview because, though her main study had been perhaps art or biology, music was her great hobby and she took care to say she had taken piano Grade VI, played for pleasure, sang in the college choir and had enjoyed helping with the percussion band on her teaching practice. Being able to play the piano, or willing to run the cubs; having accompanied the pupils on educational visits or being keen to help run the school library may be the 'qualification' that actually gets you the job! In this connection it may be worth considering particularly schools with which you may have some personal affiliation, such as religion in the case of denominational schools or your own education in a similar type of school, and there are both agencies and periodicals which may carry advertisements for such categories of schools.

First-Line Contacts
If you find yourself still without a job after you have left college, where can you get advice? Don't neglect the obvious sources:

University, College or Polytechnic Careers Advisory Service
You should be able to get help from the careers service or appointments board in the institution(s) in which you took your degree and teacher training. Universities and polytechnics have long-established services and most colleges of higher education have developed careers services within the last few years. You may be able to receive regular vacancy lists by post and if you live a long way from the institution where you graduated or trained, it may be possible to get advice or information at a nearby institution through the *mutual aid scheme*.

Local Authority Careers Service
The careers advisers are there to help those just leaving higher education as well as college students. They give careers counselling and also have information on trainee posts and other possibly suitable jobs. You will find the address of your local careers adviser in the telephone directory (under the name of the authority *or* under 'Careers Service'). Some authorities have officers who specialise in advising those with higher educational qualifications; some newly-trained teachers have been greatly helped by their careers service. In one case, after a long discussion, the teacher decided to take up a career in insurance and was successful in gaining a suitable post. In some parts of the country, however, the careers service may be under such pressure from unemployed school-leavers that it may not be able to give the level of help it would like to offer.

Job Agencies
Government Agencies
Most newly-qualified teachers seeking posts register with local Jobcentres. You are, however, also entitled to, and in my view *should*, register with Professional and Executive Recruitment (PER). There are 32 centres throughout the country and you can register by post if you are too far away to travel conveniently. Let your local Jobcentre know that you are also registering with PER. The Jobcentre will also give you the appropriate address and further information about PER. Addresses are also in the telephone directory.

The vast majority of jobs available through PER are in industry or commerce, but some of these are in fields which have proved of interest to and have employed teachers, i.e. personnel work; training officers. It handles very few teaching jobs. It does cover vacancies all over the country and all offices have details of *all* vacancies, not just the local ones.

PER operates as an employment agency, charging a fee to recruiters, and many of the vacancies registered demand relevant experience. New graduates have often, in the past, been disappointed by their approach to PER and complained they weren't sent details of any suitable posts, forgetting that a recruitment agency can only pass on the jobs that employers send them. Even if it is a long-shot in your particular job search, you should still give it a try. Can you afford to dismiss any source of help?

If you live in or around London, you should use the specialist PER unit for Graduate Appointments where staff can help you find relevant vacancies.

When you register you fill in a simple enrolment form and receive *Executive Post* weekly. This contains on average 450 vacancies (at the time of writing). You apply for those which interest you, either direct to the employer or via PER. There is a whole section devoted to personnel management and training, and another for general opportunities, which covers such things as franchises, commission-based insurance sales positions and others, as well as many interesting temporary posts under the Community Programme (CP) scheme. Recent graduates now receive a new publication *Graduate Post*. which is published in conjunction with New Opportunity Press (NOP) and is issued fortnightly. If you are registered with PER you receive the first two copies free, you pay £5.25 for the next six months and after that you receive copies free if you are still unemployed. If you are not registered with PER you can pay a personal subscription of £7.00 for six months. It is also distributed free to careers advisory services in universities and polytechnics. It lists, on average, 200 vacancies including post-graduate courses.

You can be registered with PER even whilst you are in employment, e.g. if you are still looking for something more appropriate.

Private Agencies
For certain categories of work private agencies may be helpful. Agencies in this country may not charge you a fee, as prospective employee, (i.e. the employer pays, except where extra services such as vocational guidance are accepted). Addresses of agencies dealing with teaching posts in the independent sector will be found at the end of this section. Roman Catholic teachers may be helped by the Catholic Teachers Appointments Bureau. Addresses of other employment agencies will be found in books on jobs listed in the bibliography.

Taking the Wider View
We tend to think of teaching as work in ordinary schools and you may not have thought beyond a possible diversification into the independent sector. There are, however, other possibilities. Because they are somewhat specialised they do require particular interests, strengths and possibly experience through teaching practice or chosen course options, but one of them may suit you.

Sometimes students, particularly mature students, find their first post in a special school. Most advisers would urge the intending special school teacher to work in a normal school first. But the fact remains that, because of the relative difficulty such schools have had in attracting good staff, some newly-qualified teachers with the right personal qualities and evidence (perhaps through course options or voluntary work) of real interest have been appointed.

People who have been successful in obtaining their first appointments in special schools have offered experiences like the following: voluntary work at a holiday home for the mentally handicapped; successful remedial work during teaching practice; helping handicapped children in play schemes and at special events like sports days; doing a dissertation on some aspect of special education; taking course options on the slow learner, remedial education etc; offering art or music or PE. No one such experience in itself would guarantee a favourable view of an application for a special job, but a blend of several such experiences has enabled newly-qualified teachers to break into this field.

One young graduate who trained for the first school had, whilst at school and university, done voluntary work in special schools over a period of several years. She was anxious to get a post in a special school but was restricted to a fairly narrow locality. Eventually she took a post as a nursery assistant in a nearby special school and continued to look for teaching jobs. Within the year she was appointed to a scale one teaching post in the school where she was working.

'Being a nursery assistant was the chief reason I secured the teaching post,' she said. 'It gave me the opportunity to get to know the children, which takes a long time with the severely subnormal.' As an assistant, she had the chance to teach class groups of, say, eight to ten children, an experience she felt she needed when, as a teacher, she was left completely alone with ten subnormal 16 to 19 year olds, teaching not arithmetic and reading, but coping skills such as eating at table, washing oneself, and learning how to manage in shops and on buses. She loves the work and lists the essential personal qualities not so much as having patience, but being realistic, stubborn and having 'an odd sense of humour'.

Other teachers have gone on to further training for teaching the deaf, though only one or two courses will consider inexperienced teachers. This is an area in which job prospects are comparatively good. These courses and those for experienced teachers are listed in the DES *Programme of Long Courses for Teachers*. In Scotland colleges of education may mount courses comprising attendance at a college and supervised teaching practice leading to the award of a Special Qualification for registered teachers who wish to specialise in teaching in a particular field of education. The Special Qualifications are awarded by Colleges of education and no additional period of probationery service is required; eg Special qualification as a teacher of the deaf (or visually handicapped) requires a one session full-time course at Moray House College of Education, Edinburgh. The subject of special education is treated further in Section Seven.

Boarding schools, too, both independent and the few state schools, sometimes find it hard to attract resident staff. Willingness to help with extra-curricular activities is perhaps even more important here than in the day school. The school holidays are longer than those in the maintained day sector, but staff may well have to teach on at least some Saturday mornings and take some evening preps. The ability to coach specific sports or give expert support to dramatic and musical activities, over and above one's basic subject or age-range expertise, is particularly highly valued. Teaching in a boarding school demands a much greater commitment to the community of the school but this is its very attraction for many staff. It perhaps should be mentioned that women, trained for the infant-junior age-range, may well obtain posts in boys' preparatory schools because many such schools like female teachers for the lower forms. And those who have specialist language qualifications, and have trained for juniors, may well find that this sector offers more opportunities for using their subject knowledge with young children than the maintained schools. Housemistress posts, involving duties other than teaching, are referred to elsewhere (Section Three).

Posts (both residential and non-residential) in boarding schools are advertised in the educational press, but there are organisations which help heads find staff (see Useful Addresses). The Incorporated Association of Preparatory Schools (IAPS) produces a leaflet *Teaching in Preparatory Schools* and welcomes enquiries from those seeking this type of post. Finally, I know of staff in the independent sector who have obtained posts by sending a cv with covering letter to schools in the geographical area in which they hope to teach, asking to be notified of any suitable vacancies.

Addresses of both day and boarding schools will be found in the directories *Public and Preparatory Schools Year Book* and *Girls Schools Year Book* (published by Adam and Charles Black) which should be available in public libraries.

There may be suitable vacancies, especially for graduates and those with commercial or industrial experience, in further education (FE). When full-time posts are advertised in the educational and local press, they often demand appropriate experience. As there are a few Postgraduate Certificate of Education (PGCE) courses which offer training specifically for adult education, as well as the courses leading to a Certificate in Education run by the four Further Education Teacher Training Centres, other teachers are sometimes needlessly deterred from applying for technical and further education college lectureships, but if they have relevant academic qualifications and work experience they are likely to be good candidates. In Scotland the formal qualification for teaching in further education centres is a Teaching Qualification (Further Education). While at present possession of this qualification is not a pre-requisite of employment in further education, training is desirable and in education authority establishments carries with it an addition to salary. Training is open only to persons holding a recognised appointment in further education under an employing authority and seconded to the course on full salary by that authority. It is not necessary for persons intending to teach in further education colleges to hold a TQ or to be registered with the General Teaching Council, but to be eligible for a permanent appointment the further education teacher must hold the qualifications required for admission to training as a teacher of the appropriate subject in further education colleges (1) an appropriate degree (or associateship of a central institution or other equivalent qualification). In general the minimum technical qualification is a Higher National Certificate or a Full Technological Certificate of the City and Guilds of London Institute; and (ii) relevant industrial or commercial experience; and (iii) in the Scottish Certificate of Education examination, passes on the Ordinary Grade in English and Maths. The course is offered at Jordanhill College of Education, Glasgow and consists of ten weeks full-time study at the College followed by two terms supervised teaching employment in further education and a further ten weeks full-time study.

A fairly typical example would be the geography BEd graduate with considerable experience in banking. His banking examinations, allied to his degree studies, also enabled him to offer economics as a subject. Among his other interests, he had done evening work as a part-time community worker at a local authority arts and leisure centre. The combination of these qualifications and experiences enabled him to get his first teaching post, against stiff competition, as a lecturer in business studies at a technical college — one candidate had two higher degrees! His practical banking experience was crucial (and profitable too, since it counted as related industrial experience). He is currently teaching Business and Technology Education Council

15

(BTEC) law and economics courses, and specialist professional banking subjects — the complexities of banking law and investment — which may mystify most of us. But, at the time of writing, he is also involved in other courses e.g. consumer law for young people doing a course in retailing under a Youth Opportunity Programme; the 'one part of my week where real *skill* is required in the classroom.' Elsewhere the whole base is different — 'excellent pupil motivation' for one thing! The work is hard and involves evening classes, though with time off in lieu. But like the teacher in the army a plus factor for him is the 'nice teaching environment...super people...'

Although the FE sector has also felt the cold edge of cuts, there is currently a fair amount of scope, especially for part-time work. FE has a long tradition of employing part-timers and these opportunities are often not advertised. Many tutors either build up sufficient part-time work to equate to a full-time post or use part-time experience as a route to full-time work. Tutors get involved in FE in many ways. Some have even begun as students, perhaps on a leisure craft course or taking up a new language, and happen to have the right qualifications for tutoring on another course when a vacancy occurs. Others approach their local colleges and offer to take 'O' level/grade classes in subjects for which their degree makes them appropriately qualified.

The range of subjects and level of classes in FE is very wide indeed covering leisure activities, craft and technical qualifications, courses leading to business and commercial qualifications and special courses such as those in basic literacy and numeracy for adults, or courses directed at helping married women prepare for study. *Second Chances 1983* (see bibliography) gives a vivid survey of adult FE provision. *The Directory of Further Education* lists colleges and courses.

One area of FE which is getting a major injection of funds and human resources is that of youth training. Under the New Training Initiative the aim is to offer by Autumn 1983 all 16 year old school leavers a place on the new one year foundation course currently being introduced by the Manpower Services Commission (MSC) called the Youth Training Scheme.

The programmes will vary from locality to locality but will include five core elements namely induction and assessment of trainees; skills and attainments — basic skills of literacy and numeracy as well as practical competence in using tools, office equipment, etc; work experience and block periods of training (for example at an FE college); individual guidance and counselling; and a written review of trainees' progress. Within the scheme the FE colleges have an important role. Indeed, the White Paper states 'It will mean for them a major expansion in provision for this age-group, the equivalent of perhaps 80,000 full-time places funded by the MSC.' ('A New Training Initiative: A Programme for Action'; 15 December 1981, HMSO). It will be clear from this that those with the appropriate professional skills and expertise ought to be able to find scope for their talents!

You will gather from this account that different courses will demand different combinations of expertise, experience and qualities. A teaching qualification is extremely valuable in all cases. Coupled with voluntary adult literacy tutoring, even primary training might help a teacher get work on basic numeracy and literacy courses. (Some have done so.)

On the other hand a recent mature graduate teacher with previous commercial experience might be ideal for a 'New Horizons' type course. 'New Horizons' courses, to give them only one of their names, are intended to give women, particularly housewives, the chance to reassess their skills and talents and the possibilities for training, study and employment.

Because FE can often make good use of combinations such as two or three years in industry plus a teaching qualification, new teachers who go into totally different fields have a good chance of entering education subsequently at this level.

Qualified teachers, especially those with a degree or main subject in languages or English, may consider teaching English as a foreign language (TEFL), either in this country or abroad. In Britain such teachers work in private language schools or local authority colleges. Local Education Authority (LEA) posts often demand teaching experience. Private language schools run courses for businessmen and foreign teachers of English, and also, especially in the summer, for foreign school children. The Association of Recognised English Language Schools (ARELS) produces a descriptive list of such schools. Jobs are advertised but it is also worth writing direct. Most schools want, in addition to a teaching certificate or degree, either Teaching English as a Foreign Language (TEFL) experience or a TEFL qualification.

The British Council produces lists of the short TEFL courses and the more substantial courses for the Royal Society of Arts (RSA) Certificate. The brief list is free and the detailed catalogue (1982/3 edition) is available at a cost of £1.20 (see Useful Addresses).

Useful experience can be gained initially through temporary summer course work. Some organisations taking on temporary staff are listed in the Central Bureau's publication *Working Holidays*. The Federation of English Language Course Organisations produces a booklet listing details of other such courses. You could write directly to the organisers to enquire about job opportunities.

Although RSA TEFL qualifications are widely recognised, some chains of language schools prefer to train their own staff in their own methods. These independent courses are often advertised, and before parting with any money, you should ascertain what qualification will be awarded on successful completion. Any one school's own certificate may not be acceptable outside its own organisation, and will not necessarily guarantee a job within the organisation. Reputable schools will clarify this before you join the course.

Private language schools in the UK, like any other business, suffer from such factors as a strong pound and high hotel and travel charges. These affect the number of foreign clients, and in turn the job security of the teachers.

More information on teaching English abroad will be found in the section on *Short-Term and Temporary Work*.

There are also some opportunities in the relatively new (small, but growing!) field of industrial language training. Trainers work from one of the 30 centres, usually in industrial premises, teaching English language and communication skills to immigrant workers. They design their own courses based on functional language and are also involved in training managers and shop stewards for effective communication in multiracial workplaces. The TUC takes an active interest in this work, and wherever training is provided the union is involved in the planning. Staff see themselves as rather more than language teachers, as having a role to play in fostering good personal and working relationships between people of different races. Most staff are trained teachers. Additionally they have knowledge of language and communication skills. ESL (English as a second language) or EFL experience, adult literacy work, experience of community service, work with immigrants, knowledge of industry and the trade unions are all valuable assets. Currently there are over 100 full-time trainers. Vacancies are advertised in the *TES* or *The Guardian*, though there may also be a point in applying speculatively to a local unit. The National Centre for Industrial Language Training produces a list of units and directors. The list also appears in *Second Chances 1983*.

There has also been an increasing development of education and training within industry and commerce. In most areas of this work personnel move into this function after some experience within the particular industry, but one field which the graduate teacher can enter directly is that of computers, particularly computer services. This rapidly developing industry trains graduates (including those with arts and education degrees) for a variety of functions, one of which is education. A major feature of this work is training clients in the use of computer systems. One large company recently advertised specifically for graduates *or* trained teachers for this work.

Some teachers with a suitable degree or main subjects find work in health education. This topic is dealt with in some detail in Section Seven.

Another possibility is work within the armed services. The Royal Army Education Corps (RAEC) is interested in men and women, preferably with a degree (BEd or degree plus PGCE), for short (three year) commissions as well as longer term commitments. Archaic visions of army recruitment as being offered the King's Shilling and then trapped for life prevent some people, who would in fact enjoy Education Corps work, from even enquiring! In fact, those who are accepted are on probation for six months, at the end of which they can leave if they wish. (It works the other way and they can also be fired!)

The range of work is considerable — from adult literacy to virtually degree level work. RAEC officers may work with 16-18 year olds teaching scientific subjects or liberal studies in junior soldier units; they may be tutoring officers in subjects such as international relations for their promotion examinations; perhaps teaching Russian, Chinese or Arabic to army personnel. They have opportunities to serve abroad (mainly Germany, Cyprus, Hong Kong), and also a good chance of secondment for a master's degree in order to extend their own education, or an intensive course to learn a new language. The system of seniority antedates for degrees and other qualifications makes it possible to proceed very rapidly to the rank of lieutenant, and with the right combination of letters after your name, you might even make captain in less than a year.

One young woman captain I spoke to on a visit to an education centre felt that, apart from the opportunity to travel, she appreciated having pupils who were always keen to learn. When I met her she was tutoring NCOs for their promotion exams. This gave her several subjects to teach to each new group on the four-week course. Although she was repeating the course in four-week blocks, she considered that variety was a major attraction in education corps work, since you constantly met new students and got a new posting at regular intervals, which meant a change of venue and work. In your next job you could be teaching English as a foreign language to Chinese army personnel in Hong Kong, or accompanying a Gurkha regiment as their education officer.

18

Some officers who leave the Corps after a short commission go into schools and colleges; others use the experience to move into industrial or commercial management.

Most of the teachers in schools for the children of service personnel who are abroad, are civilians. If this sort of employment, which may give you varied experience as well as foreign travel, appeals you should write to the Services Children's Education Authority (see Useful Addresses) giving details of your age-range or secondary teaching subjects and qualifications. Suitable applicants are put on a waiting list and told when a vacancy arises.

The Royal Air Force has an education specialisation within its administrative branch. Graduates who are trained teachers and can offer the physical sciences, mathematics or German were particularly being sought at the time of writing. In many ways the work is similar to that of the army education officer. Those with a BEd with main physical education or a diploma or certificate from a recognised college of physical education could enquire about the parallel physical education specialisation, although competition is likely to be very stiff, and vacancies few. Literature and further information are available at the RAF's careers information offices, and the address of your nearest one will be in the local telephone directory.

The Royal Navy also employs instructors, mainly with scientific and technical backgrounds, but the defence cuts have affected recruitment very severely.

Other organisations in which teachers may work include some residential children's homes, borstals and prisons. The posts are usually advertised in the educational press. Here again are fields where voluntary part-time or short-time work could be a relevant and valuable experience to cite when applying for jobs. The next section gives details of organisations which offer this kind of experience.

Some of the opportunities mentioned here will be included in vacancy lists obtainable from your university or college. Others will be advertised. A useful list of newspapers and periodicals will be found in *Sources of Vacancies*. The bibliography lists books which deal with careers generally.

Useful Addresses

ARELS (Association of Recognised English Language Schools)
125 High Holburn, London WC1V 6QD.

The British Council, English Teaching Information Centre
10 Spring Gardens, London SW1A 2BN.

Catholic Teachers Appointments Bureau
33 Wilfred Street, London SW1E 6PS.

FELCO (Federation of English Language Course Organisations)
43 Russell Square, London WC1B 5DG.

Gabbitas-Thring Educational Trust, Broughton House
6/8 Sackville Street, London W1X 2BR.
(posts in independent schools)
also at 63 George Street, Edinburgh EH2 2JG.

Incorporated Association of Preparatory Schools
138 Church Street, Kensington, London W8 4BN.
Secretary: J.H. Dodd; Assistant Secretary: M.P. Rawlins.
(Enquiries about vacancies should be addressed to the Assistant Secretary.)

Independent Schools Information Service
56 Buckingham Gate, London SW1E 6AG.

The International Teacher Training Institute
106 Piccadilly, London W1V 9FL.
(part of English International, an educational charitable trust, runs TEFL training courses, full-time and part-time, fee-paying)

National Centre for Industrial Language Training
The Havelock Centre, Havelock Road, Southall, Middlesex UB2 4NZ.

The Teacher
(in case of difficulty in ordering)
The Teacher Publishing Company Ltd,
Derbyshire House, Lower Street, Kettering, Northamptonshire NN16 8BB
or through newsagents.

The Truman and Knightley Educational Trust
76/78 Notting Hill Gate, London W11 3LJ.
(posts in independent schools)

Officers and Aircrew Selection Centre
Royal Air Force, Biggin Hill, Westerham, Kent TN16 3EJ.

Senior Recruiting and Liaison Officer
Royal Army Educational Corps Centre, Wilton Park, Beaconsfield, Buckinghamshire HP9 2RP.

Royal Society of Arts Examination Board
18 Adam Street, Adelphi, London WC2N 6AJ.
(information on TEFL courses)

Services Children's Education Authority
Eltham Palace, Court Road, Eltham SE9 5NR.

SHORT TERM TEMPORARY WORK TEACHING ABROAD

ASP
TESTER
WANTED
APPLY MS. CLEOPATRA

This section is of relevance to school-leavers considering time-out before going to university or college as well as those leaving degree and training courses. Experienced teachers considering work in a teaching, welfare or administrative role with a voluntary organisation will find some of the entries under voluntary work of interest, and those wanting to teach abroad will also find some useful information.

The section first considers temporary occupations as a strategy for the newly-trained who are initially unsuccessful in getting a permanent teaching job. It goes on to deal with opportunities for temporary work with children and young people, holiday and seasonal work, agency and part-time work, opportunities with voluntary organisations and working, particularly teaching, abroad. Addresses of many organisations are included in the relevant sub-sections and other useful addresses are appended to the chapter.

Temporary Measures
People who want to get a teaching post as soon as possible will probably hope for temporary work of some kind. What sort of work is available?

21

Temporary jobs in teaching itself are, of course, becoming increasingly common and are particularly valuable experience, but there are many other kinds of work you could consider. The choice obviously depends to some extent on the area where you are living, and the time of the year when you are job-hunting. Much temporary work is seasonal; it is also sensitive to general employment trends, so that in areas of high unemployment there may be little work of any sort available. You may even have to move away to get a job.

At least you can console yourself with the knowledge that we have good case-history evidence that applicants who use their time constructively impress headmasters far more than those who sit idly bemoaning their fate. Students who opt for temporary alternative work often ask, 'But will I get back into teaching after? Won't heads be suspicious of me because I've been away from the classroom? In any case, I'm worried that my confidence will be sapped, that I'll get rusty'.

Of course these are potential problems, but they would be just as real if you remained unemployed, indeed they would almost certainly be worse. Temporary work is likely at the very best to boost your self-confidence in a general way and it can offer valuable experience in dealing with people and coping with new situations. You may be able to get work that gives you experience with children that will be of positive value, as the case histories on page 14 and page 63 illustrate.

Perhaps the only thing to be said in favour of being unemployed is that after six months of it you are eligible to apply for any Community Programme (CP) job that comes to your attention.

Range of Work
Temporary vacancies do still occur in offices of all types, though the work is likely to be at the filing-clerk level unless you have a skill such as shorthand. Particularly in the pre-Christmas period large departmental stores may take on extra staff. It is worth writing direct to possible stores because they may not bother to notify the job agencies in the present circumstances. Sometimes other large firms have occasional temporary posts which do not necessarily demand specialist qualifications but need an intelligent approach. Such posts are unlikely to be advertised and the firm will probably draw from the pool of people who have written 'on spec' and expressed interest in the work of the organisation.

Working with Children and Young People
Many trained teachers feel they want to keep in touch with children in their work. In the short term it is worth considering voluntary work, for example with the Community Service Volunteers (CSV) or Voluntary Service Overseas (VSO). More detailed information on openings in this field follows later in this section.

Enterprising ex-students have sometimes made a virtue of bleak necessity by taking a temporary job abroad, for example:
to Spain to teach English in a private school
to Italy as a nursery governess in a private household
to America as a nanny
to Athens to teach English in an FE college.

If you enjoy working with young children you may find a post as a nanny an interesting way of filling the gap. Temporary posts may occur because a mother has to go into hospital or abroad for several weeks. *Nursery World* and *The Lady* specialize in advertisements in this field (posts both here and abroad). Local newspapers also carry such advertisements and sometimes the local careers officer is notified of local posts. Addresses of private registered agencies specializing in nursery posts can be found in the magazines already mentioned. You need to discuss time off, domestic arrangements and duties carefully with your prospective employer because individual households and expectations are so variable, but such work can offer an interesting experience — often profitable too because the salary is over and above board and lodging and often too the employee's share of the insurance stamp is paid by the employer. Some nanny posts are for help with school-age children and — surprising as it may seem — there are still some people able to afford nursery governesses or holidays cruising round the Greek Islands with nanny!

There is still a considerable demand for assistant housemothers and similar workers in residential children's homes, both those run by the local authorities and those run by church and other voluntary bodies. These posts are not, necessarily, very highly paid and the basic educational qualifications are much lower than a teaching qualification. Moreover, they are not usually temporary. But if you are willing to stay at least a year (i.e. before taking up a post for the next school year) you might well obtain such a post and it could offer you some attractions.

It would keep you in touch with children and give you the satisfaction of doing a worthwhile job. It will probably also ensure a roof over your head! The experience of getting to know children from difficult backgrounds will be very helpful to you when you do get your teaching post, and should you at a later date decide you want to switch to social work or to pastoral care or counselling work within the school system, you may find that the year you once thought of as biding time turns out to be a positive advantage in your career. Posts of this nature are advertised in the local press, and also the periodicals *Social Work Today* and *New Society*.

A BEd graduate, unable to get a primary post, took a job as an unqualified social worker. She was a very committed teacher, however, and a year later was concerned that the break from the classroom might be to her disadvantage when she eventually found teaching vacancies to apply for. I was able to assure her that the insights she had gained whilst working with deprived and often difficult children were a real asset. She took the practical step of arranging to spend a couple of weeks as an observer in a primary school so she no longer felt 'out of touch' when applying for teaching posts. To her delight, she found that the first school headmistress who interviewed her obviously agreed with us about the value of her experience and, indeed, she got the job.

Another residential possibility is as an assistant matron or housemistress in a boarding school. This would almost certainly be an independent school, of course, though there are some boarding schools within the state sector. The status of housemistress varies considerably. In a large public school the title may indicate a position of considerable responsibility which might well lead to deputy headship, but the term is also used for the person taking care of the general welfare of boys and girls in a boarding-house — acting as a substitute mother so that you need to have an understanding of young people, sympathy allied to firmness, commonsense and a sense of humour. The housemistress in a girls' school will supervise the girls whilst in their houses, covering roll-call, meal times and free time. She will be responsible for pocket money, visits and outings, and general pastoral care. Often in these cases no teaching is wanted but sometimes the work can include some teaching. It is worth enquiring as duties in these posts can be negotiable.

Advertisements appear in the *Times Educational Supplement* and *The Lady* also through agencies such as Gabbitas-Thring. (Address under *Looking for That First Post* above.)

The Independent Schools Information Service now runs an agency to recruit matrons and housemistresses (see Useful Addresses). It can offer both permanent and a few temporary posts. Salary scales vary depending on the duties required. They may be related to JNC scales, but any teaching element should be paid for at Burnham pro rata, or equate to the school's teaching staff's scale (which may be slightly higher than Burnham).

Holiday and Seasonal Work
Traditionally students used to sp :nd their vacations as barmaids and jolly campus friends at the big holiday camps, and the holiday industry does still offer a certain amount of scope for temporary (though also necessarily seasonal) employment.

During the holiday periods large package tour operators such as Thomsons often employ trained nursery nurses and teachers to organise activities for children of all ages in hotels abroad, whilst their parents enjoy the sun-bathing, sightseeing and wine drinking. There are, too, other companies which specialize in holidays designed for children. PGL Young Adventure Limited, a firm based in Hereford, take on annually (Easter-September) temporary personnel as instructors in various holiday activities, such as canoeing, pony-trekking, orienteering and sailing, for the school-children on their adventure holidays here and abroad.

Butlin's Ltd run School Venture Weeks for school parties at certain centres in April, May and October every year. They recruit teachers able to act as activity leaders and instructors on their support teams. Active involvement in sports, and knowledge of the rules of, say, football or volleyball are useful skills to offer, but the range of activities covers crafts, beachcombing, farm studies and map reading among others, and if you just have an 'extrovert personality' you might be the very person they want to help with initiative tests and crazy golf! The teachers accompanying the group take responsibility for the children's general welfare, behaviour etc. (See also Section Six)

Canvas Holidays recruit some 300 couriers for continental campsites (France, Spain, Italy, Switzerland) for three months in the summer. You need to be physically fit and have a high standard of conversation in the appropriate language.

Finally there are short work-camps (one to three weeks) abroad, which may provide useful experience with the elderly and mentally and physically handicapped. There are also nature conservation and play schemes. The National Youth Bureau (see Useful Addresses — Young Volunteer Resources Unit) has literature on the various schemes.

Some travel firms advertise in the educational and nursing press, but it might also be worth looking at the travel brochures and advertisements to see which companies make a feature of supervised play for young clients and then writing to see whether they can offer you any suitable employment.

Similarly some passenger shipping lines have occasional vacancies for trained nursery nurses and appropriately qualified teachers (e.g. in PE to organise the children's activities on board ship). They will almost certainly expect you to join generally in helping to entertain passengers and you may well have to act as a bingo caller or help to run a fancy-dress party. Write direct to possible shipping lines, enquiring about vacancies.

The hotel and catering trade generally still has permanent, temporary and part-time vacancies (partly, it must be admitted, because its pay structure is a great deal less attractive than say that of the Civil Service, and the hours of work are long and anti-social in the sense that its workers are often slogging away whilst the rest of the working population is relaxing over its pints and scampi — but its workers do get fed!)

There are a number of organisations which arrange language and cultural courses for foreign school-children during the holidays. See *Looking for That First Post* for further details.

There are some opportunities for travel couriers and representatives from May to mid-September on a seasonal basis. You can apply to large travel firms directly and the Institute of Travel and Tourism can give information on work in the industry. Couriers are usually over 21 and able to speak at least one European language other than English. Posts abroad, even temporary ones, tend to be competitive. Airlines and airports also often take on temporary staff in peak travel periods as ground receptionists, though opportunities are likely to be affected in the short-term by recent redundancies amongst permanent airline staff. Those with languages — sometimes less usual ones - are most in demand. In 1982 the British Airports Authority was looking for several temporary information officers for Heathrow. You needed fluent English, fluency in another language other than French — preferably Arabic, Chinese, Japanese or a Scandinavian language — and you needed to be 'of presentable appearance', helpful, patient and businesslike. There was a possibility of a permanent post at the end of six months.

All these seasonal travel and tourist jobs may appeal to those who hope to use their French (or Japanese?!) or German, somehow! A chance to use a main subject may give a temporary job an attraction which such work would not normally have for someone seeking a permanent career.

The bibliography includes some directories of temporary jobs.

Agency Work and Part-Time Work
In order to keep their options open and to be available to take a suitable permanent job whenever it occurs, some graduates, who are unable to get what they want, work for agencies supplying temporary staff. For those who do not have secretarial skills this usually means domestic work, baby-sitting, etc.

It is a way of ensuring that you can drop the temporary job at very short notice when a teaching job at least beckons. I came across one young teacher who deliberately took a job as a barmaid in a pub because it was evening work and enabled her to pick up odd days of supply teaching at a few hours' notice. But against this you must balance the nature of the work, so it is worth considering other possibilities suggested in this booklet too.

Opportunities with Voluntary Organisations
Most students who find themselves unable to get a job for some time after graduating soon discover that one of the worst aspects is the demoralising boredom they feel. Nor are their chances of getting a suitable post improved if, when they apply for it, they can say nothing more than 'unemployed' about their present situation. The time could be used constructively by working on a short-term 'contract' with a voluntary organisation. Such work may broaden your own experience, it may enable you to utilise your skills as a trained teacher and in some organisations the volunteer force is international, which is

for some volunteers an added attraction. Perhaps most important of all, you have the satisfaction of doing something useful.

A number of organisations are looking for volunteers usually for helping and caring for children, the aged, the handicapped. They may offer board and lodging and pocket money. Such work, apart from its obvious value to you, the volunteer, as a person, may be an asset when later you want to go into teaching, work for a voluntary body in a paid capacity or go into community work. Although valuable experience for would-be social workers, it is worth remembering that some social work courses which require relevant experience as a prior condition for entry will *not* accept voluntary work alone as suitable relevant experience.

Many voluntary bodies have said they would give a warm welcome to any unemployed teachers offering their services. Details of some organisations likely to appeal particularly to teachers follow. I have included a few organisations where posts are not of the residential/pocket money type for those who may perforce have to spend a period unemployed at home.

A very useful *Volunteer Bureaux Directory* for those who want to see what openings are available in their home locality is published by the Volunteer Centre. (See Useful Addresses.)

National Cyrenians
National Cyrenians is an association of 26 affiliated groups which run houses, day centres and night shelters for single homeless people throughout the country.

National Cyrenians aims 'to provide a positive alternative to large, rigidly organised hostels and more traditional social work attitudes. Our houses are not run by wardens but by the people (workers and residents) who live in them. They are generally small with between 8 and 15 residents. We accept individuals as they are and as they would like to be — not imposing our solutions and standards upon them.'

The association offers a valuable opportunity to do something very different before embarking on a career in, say, nursing, social work or the probation service. Volunteers work on a project for, on average, 6-9 months and are usually aged between 18 and 35 years.
For more information: Volunteers Secretary, National Cyrenians, 13 Wincheap, Canterbury, Kent CT1 3TB.

International Voluntary Service
'IVS provides the most complete range of types of voluntary service of any charity in Britain. It runs International Workcamps in Britain throughout the year but especially between late June and early September and at Christmas and Easter, and in Europe mainly in the Summer. They normally last between two and three weeks and include such work as helping in psychiatric hospitals, assisting with holidays for handicapped children, running children's playschemes and working with minority groups. IVS also provides opportunities for longer term voluntary service from six months to two years in Britain and Europe and for a minimum of two years in the Third World.'
For more information: IVS, Ceresole House, 53 Regent Road, Leicester LE1 6YL for full details including conditions, requirements and application forms for the full range of voluntary service.

The Ockenden Venture
The Venture has vacancies at its homes in Haslemere and Camberley. Helpers come from a variety of countries; at present they include Danish, Dutch and British volunteers. They receive hundreds of requests for placement so apply well in advance. 'A prime object of the community is to provide an alternative method of education and practical training' for young refugees from abroad as well as adolescent English children on care orders from local authorities. Volunteers must be willing to share completely in the life of the houses, including domestic chores. Board and lodging and minimum pocket money of £10.00 per week increasing on a sliding scale depending on age, experience and qualifications. Opportunities often exist for people with ESL qualifications to teach refugee children.
For more information: Miss N Muller, The Ockenden Venture, Guildford Road, Woking GU22 7UU.

The Salvation Army Service Corps
For Christians who are prepared to give a fixed period of full-time service. Service in the United Kingdom is mainly of a social and community character. Overseas service is restricted to those with professional competence willing to offer three years. Adherence to the Army's position re teetotalism and non-smoking required during period of service.
For more information: The S A Service Corps Officer, 101 Queen Victoria Street, London EC4P 4EP.

The Sue Ryder Foundation
Homes founded by Lady Ryder of Warsaw; exist primarily for the incurably sick and disabled, though many also admit temporary patients. The aim is to give patients 'a family sense of being at home.' In Britain the Foundation would welcome ex-student teachers willing to work at least a month, and preferably longer. They can offer some opportunities for temporary employment as well as accepting suitable people willing to offer their service on a voluntary basis. The Foundation tells us that 'the work involved is varied, and can range from cleaning and cooking to the care of the patients, to secretarial and other work assisting Lady Ryder's small team at the Foundation's headquarters in Suffolk.' Interested applicants are strongly advised to read Lady Ryder's autobiography *And the Morrow is Theirs*. This gives an insight into the ideals and activities of the Foundation.
For more information: Sue Ryder Foundation, Cavendish, Suffolk CO10 8AY.

Time for God
Full-time voluntary service, three to twelve months in church and community, operated jointly by Baptists, Church of England, United Reformed Church and the Methodist Association of Youth Clubs. Varied work with young people, children, handicapped and elderly. Full board, £12 pocket money, return fares home including one week-end each three months.
For more information: Time for God Office, Free Church Federal Council, 27 Tavistock Square, London WC1H 9HH.

National Association for the Welfare of Children in Hospital
Voluntary opportunities vary greatly from area to area. Where groups exist there is plenty of scope for volunteers. A geographical list of groups is available at Head Office.
For more information: Mrs Naomi Bradley, General Administration, NAWCH, Exton House, 7 Exton Street, London SE1 8UE.

The Boys' Brigade
Celebrates its centenary year in 1983. Uniformed boys' organisation of which each company is part of a Christian church. Some opportunity for those able to instruct in sporting and other skills and take classes. The Annual Report lists names and addresses of regional full-time officials.
For more information: Head Office, Brigade House, Parsons Green, London SW6 4TH.

The Society of Voluntary Associates
Based in London area. Voluntary work with offenders, ex-offenders and their families. Works in association with the probation service. Work includes adult literacy and youth work as well as prison visits.
For more information: SOVA, 240a Clapham Road, London SW9 0PZ.

The Leonard Cheshire Foundation
Voluntary workers for domestic tasks and to assist in the general care of residents who need personal help, including help with hobbies, letter writing, etc. Most call for help during holiday months (when permanent staff on holiday). Free board and lodging, pocket money, currently £13 per week. Minimum one month.

Also *paid posts* as assistants to trained staff.
For more information: Personnel Adviser, The Leonard Cheshire Foundation, Leonard Cheshire House, 26/9 Maunsel Street, London SW1P 2QN.

Camphill Communities
Rudolph Steiner homes, schools and villages and training centres for maladjusted, retarded, and mentally handicapped children and adults. The centres are run on a communal basis. Short-term volunteer helpers from Britain and abroad can stay six months to one year. A list of centres etc. is available.
For more information: Miss Ann Harris, Secretary, The Camphill Village Trust, Delrow House, Hilfield Lane, Aldenham, Watford WD2 8DJ.

Community Service Volunteers
Arranges projects for full-time volunteers up to the age of 35 all over the British Isles. Can make use of special talents, e.g. in sports or crafts. Prefer volunteers who offer a year, but will accept commitment for minimum of four months. Projects varied and include work in schools, borstals, community art groups, with mentally and physically handicapped, etc. Travel expenses to and from project, board and lodging if away from home plus spending money.
For more information: CSV, 237 Pentonville Road, London N1 9NJ.

Adult Literacy
Would be tutors can be put in touch with local schemes via the referral service. Voluntary work can sometimes lead to paid employment in this field.
In England write to: Referral service, 252 Western Avenue, London W3 6XJ.
In Scotland: Network, Dowanhill, 74 Victoria Crescent Road, Glasgow G12 9JQ.
In Northern Ireland: Reading and Writing Help Service (Northern Ireland), Room 208, Bryson House, 28 Bedford Street, Belfast BT2 7FE.

Church of England Children's Society
Sometimes has temporary or part-time vacancies at head office and some establishments welcome voluntary help.

Also occasional *paid posts* as e.g. teachers in London schools for handicapped and maladjusted, nursery assistants at day care centres, assistant (unqualified) residential social workers and as appeals staff.

For more information: Personnel Officer, Church of England Children's Society, Old Town Hall, Kennington Road, London SE11 4QD.

Working Abroad

Those considering going abroad in search of work are probably thinking of two possibilities; either looking for a teaching post, perhaps in a voluntary capacity, or for short-term temporary work. Some of the books and pamphlets listed in the bibliography will give much more information than can be given in a guide of this size, but the following notes may be useful.

In European countries and the USA and Canada it is extremely difficult for British teachers with British qualifications to obtain posts in state schools because most countries have requirements of nationality and national qualification. There are, however, a few posts available under the Foreign Language Assistants Exchange Scheme as English language assistants. The scheme is run by the Central Bureau for Educational Visits and Exchanges. The Folk University of Sweden annually recruits British teachers for adult education work. Experienced teachers will find both the Central Bureau and the British Council run exchange schemes for which they may well be eligible.

It is possible to obtain a post in an independent school abroad since the strict requirements of nationality and qualification may not apply. There are a few schools where English is the medium of teaching. Posts may be advertised in *The Times Educational Supplement* or you may write direct to the institutions which interest you. The Swiss National Tourist Office, for example, publishes a list of boarding and day schools in Switzerland offering British or American schools' curriculum. Similarly the Royal Netherlands Embassy produces a list of Dutch schools where tuition is given in English. It is always worth writing to the Embassy of any country which interests you.

The European Council of International Schools is an organisation of more than 100 independent international schools. It produces a newsletter and annual directory of English-language international schools. Individual members paying the full subscription (currently £40 for 12 months for initial year) receive publications, and are entitled to use the placement and relocation service. ECIS says there are normally several hundred openings for teachers in their member schools annually, although 'few appointments are made of candidates with less than two years of experience at the appropriate age or grade level'.

Another possibility is to work as a teacher of English as a foreign language in a language school abroad. Some schools advertise in directories such as *Graduate Opportunities (GO)*, *Directory of Opportunities for Graduates (DOG)* and *Graduate Employment and Training (GET)*. Increasingly the better established English Language Schools look for graduates or graduate teachers with a Teaching English as a Foreign Language qualification. In some schools the teaching may be entirely by the direct method which can be exhausting.

The British Schools Group recruits for language schools in Italy, and both Inlingua and Linguarama are among the regular recruiters of teachers and graduates for schools in Europe. Teacher training is always an advantage and the degree discipline is not important. Inlingua and Linguarama recruit for the TEFL courses they run themselves, but successful completion of the course does not guarantee a job.

A few years ago the developing countries offered many opportunities to graduates and qualified teachers at all levels of their education systems. Although these countries are now pursuing a policy of employing their own nationals as teachers, there are, nevertheless, good opportunities in secondary schools — in particular for those offering mathematics, science and English, home economics, agricultural science, and technical and commercial subjects.

The Overseas Development Administration is one of the largest recruiters but virtually all its posts are for *experienced* qualified teachers. Voluntary Service Overseas has openings for newly-trained as well as experienced teachers.

Christians Abroad produces a particularly helpful and sometimes thought-provoking series of information sheets, which anyone contemplating work in the Third World would be well advised to read. For details of these see entry under *Programmes and Vacancies*. The leaflets indicate the changing attitudes that have developed towards Western volunteers in recent years. It is worth reminding teachers that they may find schools in Africa, for example, somewhat limited and rigid in their syllabus and teaching methods compared with their British counterparts. Among the qualities the prospective volunteer may need are adaptability, being able to live with some degree of insecurity, resourcefulness and 'stickability — a readiness to take the rough with the smooth'.

Programmes and Vacancies

Christians Abroad
Operates on behalf of the Ministry of Overseas Development, High Commissions of Nigeria, Zambia and Jamaica, Anglican, Roman Catholic and United Churches in Nigeria and mission agencies in a number of countries. Receives applications, takes up references and conducts interviews leading to recommendations for appointments. Up-to-date lists of vacancies in secondary schools on both salaried and missionary (volunteer) terms can be obtained from the address below. A set of leaflets entitled *A Place For You Overseas* can be sent for £1.00. Individual leaflets (e.g. on *Secondary Education* or *Tertiary and Teacher Education*) can be sent for the cost of a postage stamp. Enquirers should send brief particulars of their qualifications, interests and experience and send stamps to cover the return postage. Most posts require a degree and teaching qualification (or BEd). English, mathematics, science are the most widely sought specializations. There is almost no call nowadays for foreign primary staff. Such opportunities as there are with this age-range are advertised in *The Times Educational Supplement*.
For more information: Christians Abroad, 15 Tufton Street, London SW1P 3QQ.

The Council for World Mission
The Council for World Mission has details of opportunities for graduate and non-graduate secondary teachers in a variety of countries abroad, e.g. Papua New Guinea, 'Teachers needed for United Church's four High schools .... specialist experience in Science or English'. Although they prefer teachers with two years experience, we have contacted the Council and they say they are willing to consider newly-qualified teachers with secondary school teaching practice experience.
For more information: The Personnel Secretary, World Church and Mission Department, United Reformed Church, 86 Tavistock Place, London WC1H 9RT.

British Volunteer Programme
Anticipates requests for volunteers from a wide range of countries in Africa, Asia, Latin America, the Caribbean and the Pacific area. It provides a framework for four organisations:
CIIR Overseas Volunteeers, International Voluntary Service, United Nations Association and Voluntary Service Overseas. Volunteers are normally over 21 (no upper age limit) and willing to serve for a minimum of two years. Final year students are advised to apply early in their last academic year. A teaching certificate or diploma is a recognised qualification and 50% of the volunteers are teachers, usually sent via VSO. Volunteers receive accommodation and payment related to local salary conditions. Appropriate travel costs are met and a small resettlement grant is paid on return home. Couples without dependent children can be posted together provided both have appropriate skills and qualifications and are selected as suitable volunteers.
For more information: The Secretary, British Volunteer Programme, 2 Cambridge Terrace, London NW1 4JL.

Voluntary Service Overseas
Welcomes trained teachers to serve in Third World countries. Recruits over 200 teachers annually. Currently recruitment is predominantly for secondary maths and sciences and English. Modern language teachers interested in English as a foreign language would be welcome for certain posts. There are also TEFL adult education posts. Although primary teachers are not recruited for primary posts, *experienced* primary teachers are wanted for teacher training posts. Early application is advisable.
For more information: VSO, 9 Belgrave Square, London SW1X 8PW.

Folk University of Sweden
The British Centre, in 1982/3, expects to recruit approximately 40 new teachers for English as a foreign language, mainly in adult education, though possibly a few hours per week in secondary schools. Teachers are expected to stay for at least a full academic year. For tax reasons it is advisable to stay for more than one year and less than two. These are posts paid at professional rates.
For more information: Mr Michael Wills, International Language Services, 14 Rollestone Street, Salisbury, Wiltshire SP1 1ED.

Church Missionary Society
Takes Christians, as both missionaries and volunteers, to work in many parts of Africa and Asia. In autumn 1981 it was seeking 100 people to work in the education and pastoral and theological fields.
For more information: Overseas Service Dept., Church Missionary Society, 157 Waterloo Road, London SE1 8UU.

Interservice
An information service which puts evangelical Christians hoping to serve abroad (or in the UK) in touch with organisations seeking their skills and abilities. Operates in conjunction with the Evangelical Alliance and the Evangelical Missionary Alliance.
For more information: Interservice, 19 Draycott Place, London SW3 2SJ.

Japanese Government English Teaching Recruitment Programme
In 1983 43 UK nationals (single, under 30 years of age, graduates) will be recruited as teaching assistants of EFL to work in secondary schools, technical schools, universities and private companies. Degree essential, teaching qualification an advantage. Successful applicants must acquire basic Japanese through the scheme's course before

departure. Fares paid, salaried.
For more information: Recruitment Officer, Japan Information Centre, 9 Grosvenor Square, London W1X 9LB.

Short-term Jobs Abroad
Apart from the volunteer programmes for teachers, there are short-term vacancies for volunteers abroad on similar lines to the schemes listed in the section above on *Voluntary Work*. The details given below relate to such a scheme and are offered as an example. Vacation Work Press publishes regular bulletins of summer jobs in Britain and abroad, as does the Central Bureau.

Concordia
Short-term summer work camps abroad for people normally between ages 18 and 25, in some cases up to 30. Mainly European — in forestry, conservation schemes, etc, so you need to be physically fit. Some opportunities for archaeological work in Italy for students of the subject. Also paid work in the wine harvest in France and Germany. For more information: The Recruitment Secretary, 8 Brunswick Place, Hove, Sussex BN3 1ET.

Invest in Yourself
If you still have time on your hands and a little money in your pocket, don't spend it all studying the pools and waiting for the draws — not unless you were born lucky!

Invest something in a new skill. Learn to drive or to type, improve your recorder playing, learn to speak Urdu or Norwegian, get some practice with computers. Whenever I tell that to final-year students, I get an initial reaction of laughter, but on reflection people see it makes sense.

Come the spring term some married woman is bound to tell me, 'I've started driving lessons already. Now I'm looking at job ads. I realize that if I can drive, I can think in terms of teaching in rural schools off the bus routes, or travel twenty miles from home in the same time it would take to do half that by public transport. So I am now able to apply for jobs that were once ruled out on grounds of distance alone'. Or in the autumn someone will wail, 'I just need a temporary job near my fiancé, but I've been looking for months. All the jobs in the Jobcentre seem to need someone who can type or drive'.

Almost no skill you acquire will be without value. As you read this book you will come across many jobs which want interesting and unusual mixtures of talents and experience. Unless you have a very high level of self-discipline, however, I should advise you to take a course of some kind. Otherwise, especially if you are unemployed, the sheer amount of time available makes it hard to stick to the task you have set yourself. See *Second Chances 1983, The Directory of Further Education* and *Directory of Independent Training and Tutorial Organisations* for information on the wealth of adult education and training opportunities. All these books are listed in the bibliography.

Community Enterprise Programme
From time to time your local Jobcentre may have interesting temporary posts available for which you are eligible if you have been unemployed for six months. These are probably posts funded via MSC under a scheme such as Community Programme (CP). A number of newly-trained teachers have obtained very useful experience in areas such as conservation, museum work and social work in this way. These posts are also sometimes advertised in the appropriate periodicals and are included in *Executive Post*. The six months rule can be interpreted very strictly and I have known applicants ruled as ineligible because they have had a few days' supply work.

Useful Addresses

The British Council
10 Spring Gardens, London SW1A 2BN.

British Schools Group
Viale Liegi 14, Rome 00198, Italy.

Butlin's Ltd (Schools Venture Weeks)
21 Southernhay West, Exeter EX1 1PR.

Courier Recruitment Manager, Canvas Holidays Ltd
Bull Plain, Hertford SG14 1DY.

Central Bureau for Educational Visits and Exchanges
Seymour Mews House, Seymour Mews, London W1H 9PE and 3/4 Bruntsfield Cres,
Edinburgh EH10 4EZ.

European Council of International Schools
18 Lavant Street, Petersfield, Hampshire GU32 3EW.

Inlingua Teacher Service
50 Fitzroy Street, London W1P 5HS.

Institute of Travel and Tourism
53/4 Newman Street, London W1P 4JJ.

ISIS Care Agency
36-38 Red Lion Street, Alvechurch, Birmingham B48 7LF.
(agency for matron and housemistress jobs in the independent sector)

Linguarama Ltd
53 Pall Mall, London SW1Y 5JH.

National Association of Voluntary Hostels
33 Long Acre, London WC2E 9LA.

Overseas Development Administration
Eland House, Stag Place, London SW1E 5DH.

PGL Young Adventure Ltd
Station Street, Ross-on-Wye, Herefordshire HR9 7AH.

Vacation Work
9 Park End Street, Oxford OX1 1HJ.

Volunteer Centre
29 Lower Kings Road, Berkhampstead, Hertfordshire HP4 2HB.

Young Volunteer Resources Unit, National Youth Bureau
17/23 Albion Street, Leicester LE1 6GD.
(for guidance on voluntary openings)

Voluntary Work in Scotland
Information from: Scottish Council for Social Services, 18/19 Claremont Crescent, Edinburgh EH7 4QD

FINDING A NEW STARTING POINT

This section is concerned with possibilities of permanent posts in other professional or junior executive fields for the young certificated teacher. Many of the suggestions are, of course, equally applicable to the qualified teacher with a degree and I have included examples appropriate to both. The experienced teacher without a degree will find many of the suggestions relevant but should also consult Section Six, which deals with the general problems specific to the older career changer. Section Seven explores careers for which *experience* of teaching is essential or particularly valuable.

This section begins by outlining the important questions you should consider before pursuing an alternative career. It then looks at the value to other employers of the teaching qualification as such; looking first at careers where the qualification is directly useful, and then at careers for which it may have developed the relevant skills.

Things to Consider

Although many of the jobs suggested under *Short-Term and Temporary Work* could lead to a new career, here we are concerned with the nub of the question: *What can a teacher do except teach?*

The experienced teacher and the mature student have an interesting range of opportunities in other fields and these are considered in another section. The crucial point is that such opportunities depend upon the *experience* rather than the *initial qualification* so that the position of the new college-leaver is very different from that of his friend with even as little as two or three years in schools.

There are three things you should do when considering other possibilities.

— Try to assess honestly the qualities and skills you can offer an employer.
— Explore the range of careers open to you so that you can make an informed decision.
— Decide whether you are seriously looking for a new direction or whether you are really treating another job as a stop-gap.

This last point is one you can reach only when you have explored the realistic possibilities, but I am treating it first here because it is a vital factor in determining the attitude of employers. When teaching jobs first became scarce, a number of students found employers sympathetic to the plight of teachers but wary of taking them on the pay-roll, because they feared that after an expensive training these employees would leave the moment a suitable teaching job turned up. You may have to work hard to convince an employer that you *do* want to be a civil servant or a salesman *despite* your training as a teacher. If you can't convince yourself, it may be better to do as students in the past have done and get a stop-gap job as a petrol-pump attendant or painting boats, where the employer has less outlay in training terms and is more willing to accept that you will leave at short notice.

What is My Teaching Qualification Worth?

One of the first questions student teachers often ask is 'What else does my certificate qualify me to do?' I indicate elsewhere that the answer may be at first sight depressing. There are indeed —

Some Careers Where the Teaching Qualification May Be Directly Useful

If you satisfactorily completed the requirements of the Secretary of State for Education and Science for the status of qualified teacher, you are also qualified to be a *youth worker or community centre warden* (except in Scotland). This is a developing careers area and there are possibilities of a combined teacher-youth worker or teacher-warden role and, for the experienced person, this can reach the head of department, even principal level. Apart from posts as community youth worker, or community centre warden, there is a range of other work. Most youth workers are employed by local authorities but a substantial minority work for voluntary organisations.

The Young Mens' Christian Association (YMCA) for example recruits teachers to its full-time staff to work as assistants in youth and community programmes. Experience of youth work is always an advantage. Typical qualities asked for in youth work advertisements, apart from relevant experience, are 'ability to work on own initiative', 'sensitivity' and for some posts 'administrative ability'.

Some local authority posts ask specifically for youth and community training and there are shortened one-year courses available (e.g. at Westhill College) for which teachers are eligible.

The National Youth Bureau publishes a useful descriptive pamphlet called *Training for Professional Youth and Community Work* which details all courses. Posts are advertised in *Youth and Community, Social Work Today* and *Youth Service Appointments* and the journal *New Society* also carries advertisements for this type of post, as do *The Times Educational Supplement* and *Community Care*. Try *Time Out* too. In Scotland, information on this type of work is available from the Scottish Community Education Centre.

If you are a qualified PE teacher you may be eligible for a shortened course to train as a *remedial gymnast*. Remedial gymnasts work in hospitals and rehabilitation centres with patients suffering from both physical and mental illnesses. The work, which involves active exercise for patients, ranges from organising games planned to encourage competition as an aid to more rapid recovery, to helping a patient to use an artificial limb. Courses are run at the College of Remedial Gymnasts and Recreational Therapy, Pinderfields General Hospital, Aberford Road, Wakefield, West Yorkshire WF14DG, and at the University Hospital of Wales, Heath Park, Cardiff CF44XW. Posts are advertised in the journal of the Society of Remedial Gymnastics. Salary scales now offer a very good career structure.

In a similar way qualified home economics teachers, who also have a minimum of seven 'O' levels/grades including chemistry, are eligible for a shortened course to train as a *dietitian*. Trained home economists sometimes obtain posts as demonstrators, advisers or lecturers for food manufacturers and bodies such as the Gas and Electricity Boards.

A field to which many experienced PE teachers have moved is *recreation management*. This is a relatively new career with a fairly flexible level of entry still and a fluid career pattern. Many of the personnel are employed by local authorities but there are opportunities in the private sector too. One young man, now working for a London borough as a recreation officer, finds his teacher training directly relevant in the small amount of work he does coaching games within youth clubs and play schemes, but what he really enjoys about the work is the challenge of organising and planning activities.

Posts are advertised in the local and national press and in *Opportunities*, and if your own institution, like mine, has a strong PE department you may well find that they, or the Careers Service, hear of posts from time to time — an assistant manager at a sports centre, for example. Although some coaching may be required, administrative abilities are even more important than sporting prowess. Useful assets for the newly qualified teacher are life-saving qualifications, experience of running a bar, part-time or vacation jobs at, for instance, a swimming-bath, willingness to work evenings and at weekends, and a willingness to 'muck in'. If other staff are off sick it may be you acting as barman or humping equipment — even, in an emergency, unblocking the loos!

'Recreation' isn't just about conventional sports these days and local authority centres as well as independent ones may have to operate profitably. There may be exhibition and concert halls for which to arrange lettings, as well as swimming-pools and squash courts, and commercial expertise will be demanded.

A typical centre advertising for experienced staff described its aim as 'to achieve a balance between sport, art and entertainment'. So those with interests in the field of the creative arts and museum work might also consider this type of work since many local authorities bring galleries and museums under the same administrative umbrella as sports stadiums. On the other hand many stately homes are sprouting leisure activities such as boating and riding in their surrounding parklands.

One PE teacher got his first job working as a leisure officer for a large theme park run by private enterprise. In addition to his sporting interests and lively, outgoing personality he was able to offer an interesting background of vacation and part-time jobs, from commentating at an agricultural show to helping run medieval banquets. Little did he think where leading the revels might eventually take him!

Some Careers Relating to Teaching
There are a number of careers which may be seen as related to teaching either because knowledge and experience of teaching is an asset in the job or because they are in the educational world, or simply because they require many of the qualities a teacher also needs. Students unable to find work in teaching may naturally turn to these fields first. They feel safer on more familiar ground and have a comforting sense that they haven't wasted all that training. Unfortunately, some of the jobs that may be most appealing require *experience* of teaching rather than qualified teacher status. *Switching to a New Field* will give you further information on these 'second careers'.

Jobs such as that of a nanny or a school housemistress have been referred to elsewhere. Here are some others where work with the young may be involved or where the 'helping' element is strong.

Educational Welfare Officers have as their chief responsibility the enforcing of school attendance. The work demands a certain maturity and some older students who trained as teachers have taken posts in this field. I have, however, known of at least one young BEd graduate who moved into this field only a year or so after qualifying. She had followed courses within her degree that were relevant to social work and she had the right personal qualities. Those interested in this work should apply to the Chief Education Welfare Officer in the districts where they hope to work. Posts are also sometimes advertised in social work journals and *Opportunities*. Advertisements sometimes mention a teaching qualification as a useful asset. Selection boards usually look for the appropriate personal qualities rather than academic knowledge — perceptive, sensitive, but also firm and tough-minded, and able to communicate with everyone from court officials to truculent parents.

Social work is a career which seems to call on some of the qualities which trained teachers might well possess. The recognised qualification is either the two-year Certificate of Qualification in Social Work (CQSW) course or a postgraduate diploma. For the one-year diploma applicants must possess a 'relevant' degree. What is classified as 'relevant' varies from institution to institution but it usually requires study of social administration. If you do not possess a 'relevant' social science degree, you can take a one-year postgraduate social science diploma course which qualifies you for the one-year training instead. Appropriate work experience is a prerequisite. But taking a job to gain experience of life and then applying for the non-graduate course is still seen as a very valid way of entering this career.

There are some opportunities for college and university leavers to gain experience as social work assistants with local authorities. Some courses will accept students who have suitable experience with a voluntary organisation. Work as a residential child care officer would also be acceptable. It is certainly true that maturity and 'experience of life' are valuable assets for any would-be social worker, and those considering this career may be advised to see it as a 'second career' rather than an alternative to teaching. Local authorities have in the past offered a number of posts to new graduates as trainee social workers. These jobs guaranteed secondment to a suitable course leading to qualified social worker status. The cuts in public expenditure have drastically reduced the number of these openings, but some authorities, unable to guarantee secondment, still see it as a priority for new assistants.

In its leaflet advising pupils at school on how to 'Plan Ahead for a Career in Social Work', Central Council for Education and Training in Social Work (CCETSW) makes a very pertinent point: 'General life experience can be widened in any job and at the same time experience of helping people can be gained from voluntary work.' So *any* experience can be useful, but if you decide to move into this field permanently, you will eventually want to gain experience which will fulfill the pre-course requirements.

Some voluntary bodies, such as the Richmond Fellowship, recruit graduates and others to train (in this case to work in their communities for the mentally ill).

The probation service (in England and Wales only) and prison service may interest some teachers, because they offer some opportunities for working with young people. The recognised qualification for probation officers is the CQSW. The Home Office sponsors a number of trainee posts for those taking CQSW courses approved for probation service training, and who intend to work as probation officers. Those sponsored in this way are paid a salary, not a grant. The number of trainee posts, at any one time, depends upon estimates of the vacancies in the service for the newly qualified and it can vary from year to year. (See Useful Addresses for both CCETSW and Home Office sponsorships.) Leaflets should be available in Careers Offices. Other social work trainees, apart from those on secondment, depend on the discretionary awards, which are likely to be few and far between in the immediate future.

Appointment to Assistant Governorship Class II in the Prison Service is open to suitable applicants with a good higher education, and an increasing number of graduates is entering the service. One mature student, who was successful in obtaining direct entry to prison management through this scheme, had been a psychiatric nurse before she trained to teach. Unable to obtain a teaching post on qualifying, she looked around for other possibilities. Most of the rival candidates for assistant governorship were serving prison officers and she had to convince the selectors of her interest in this sort of work. The organisational aspects of her training are useful, and her previous work as a nurse is often relevant. The communication skills and ability to 'get on with people', which her teacher training developed, are vital in her new role and, of course, she will take a particular interest in education within her institution. Like the special school and FE teachers mentioned in Section Two , at this stage in her career, she stressed more the differences between teaching and what she is doing now. But hearing the detailed descriptions of her work, one can see evidence of many transferable skills.

Play leadership is a very different type of career which involves work with the young. The National Playing Fields Association has published a very useful *NPFA Play and Volunteer Directory* listing play facilities and opportunities and covering more than 5000 play schemes. Perhaps of most use to the volunteer or temporary worker, it should nevertheless prove helpful to someone hoping to make a career in the field. The Directory is available in one volume and in separate regional editions from the NPFA.

There are other jobs which relate somewhat tangentially to teaching; educators visiting schools and factories to support road safety and accident prevention, for example. A recent advertisement for an assistant accident prevention officer in a London borough asked for 'a pleasant personality', ability 'to communicate effectively with people of all age groups', administrative skills and a driving licence — essential this last! The person appointed would be helping with a programme of education, training and publicity covering road, home and water safety.

There are administrative posts within charitable bodies. Charity administration is considered in more detail in Section Seven, since it often suits older people. There are, however, some openings for the newly qualified. A typical job might be the one advertising for two administrative assistants, graduate or non-graduate, to work for a charity helping the dependents of prisoners. Basic typing was essential and personal qualities sought included 'tact and sensitivity', the ability to communicate with all sorts of people and to negotiate welfare rights on behalf of families.

A knowledge of schools is obviously valuable in any work which relates to the production of educational resources or to the organisation of the education system. Educational administration is one such area which does absorb a small number of new graduates each year (not necessarily trained teachers, of course). Openings exist in local education authorities for administrative trainees and, from time to time, in colleges, polytechnics and universities. It will be obvious, however, that the closure of colleges of education and the economies likely to be imposed on LEAs this year will mean that opportunities in these fields will be severely restricted.

Occasional openings occur with the examining boards or with an organisation such as the Central Clearing House. Section Seven deals with this career in further detail.

Other fields related to education either recruit experienced teachers or people with another type of expertise e.g. almost all educational journalists (as opposed to freelance contributors) are primarily journalists who happen to specialize in education; field centre and outdoor pursuits centre staff have, often in addition to teaching qualifications, particular botanical or other scientific expertise or high-level skills in the appropriate sporting pursuits.

Careers such as educational publishing and the museum service, though they may annually offer a handful of vacancies to the college leaver or graduate, are dealt with more appropriately in *Switching to a New Field*.

What Have You to Offer?

Although the opportunities suggested above may seem restricted, the picture is much more optimistic if the question about the value of teacher training is looked at in another way. Instead of asking, 'What is the qualification worth?' you could ask, 'What knowledge, skills and personal qualities have I acquired and developed during my years at college?'

Teachers as a group are (despite the adverse publicity from time to time!) reliable and responsible people. You have already demonstrated your motivation for a career by training for a profession.

As part of your training you have undertaken work experience (teaching practice) which has been assessed. You have proved you can organise a work schedule, make plans and modify them in the light of experience, organise a group of 30 or more children, fit into an existing institution and get on with your colleagues.

It is quite possible to gain a degree, at least in some subjects, whilst leading an introverted and isolated existence, working alone perhaps in libraries. It is impossible to qualify as a teacher without demonstrating some strength of social skills, and the ability to communicate verbally and in writing. Probably also you have engaged successfully in some kind of team project.

All these qualities and skills are marketable — indeed, they are very much in demand.

The suggestions which follow below and in the next section are by no means exhaustive. All are in fields in which I know teachers have obtained posts and, in a number of cases, employers have actively sought teachers.

If you studied English or mathematics, you may be particularly welcome by insurance companies. A number of leavers every year have taken up this type of work, not on the sales side but as general trainees.

The ability to communicate and to work well with other people are both qualities many employers value and which many (perhaps most) teachers feel they possess. On the strength of such personal qualities some have moved into personnel work in industry. Public relations, customer liaison and quality control are also fields in which these qualities are vital.

Sales, particularly if your subject or your interest in education and children is relevant to the business, is obviously a possibility for people who can talk easily to others and explain things clearly. For example, pharmaceutical firms seeking medical represent- atives have specifically mentioned that the job might appeal to teachers, especially if they have a scientific background.

Work for a play equipment manufacturer might similarly relate to the courses you have studied.

Some areas of work where a particular kind of mind can be trained in a comparatively short time may offer possibilities to the trained teacher. Computer firms, for instance, have found that teachers with 'O' level mathematics but not necessarily any higher study of the subject have proved successful as *computer programmers*. (Not all such teachers, of course, would have the right aptitudes for this career.) This is a field which offers considerable career opportunities.

The Computing Service Association has produced a *Directory of Members and Services* which, though not a directory of current recruiters, may provide useful background information for those making speculative applications or wanting to know more about a name in an advertisement. It may well be available in your college or university careers library.

The National Computing Centre produces careers literature. (See Useful Addresses.)

Technical writers are also sometimes recruited from amongst the ranks of teachers, since the ability to express what is often complex material in clear and accurate language is one of the requirements of the job. Science and English are useful subjects, but it must be remembered that some firms want their technical writers to produce manuals, instructions and so on for the specialist rather than the layman, and they will be looking for, say, engineers who just happen to be able to write as well!

If you are interested in any of these careers, consult some of the books in the bibliography. You will also find in these books addresses of potential employers and professional institutions.

Once you stop thinking in terms of careers for a teacher and start thinking in terms of a career for *you* — you as an individual who just happens to have a teaching qualification in addition to all your other assets and attributes — the field becomes very wide.

The next section explores this question further in the discussion of the certificate and the value of an 'any discipline' degree, and *What Teachers Did* illustrates how wide the range of possibilities can be.

Useful Addresses

CCETSW Information Service
Derbyshire House, St Chad's Street, London WC1H8AD*also at* 9 South St David Street, Edinburgh EH22BY.
(information on social work, training courses, etc.)

Clearing House for CQSW Courses
4th Floor, Myson House, Railway Terrace, Rugby, Warwickshire CV213HT

Computing Services Association
5th Floor, Hanover House, 73/4 High Holburn, London WC1V6LE.

Criminal Police Department
Room 256, 50 Queen Anne's Gate, London SW1H9AT.
(probation training sponsorship) (For England and Wales)

National Computing Centre
Oxford Road, Manchester M17ED.

National Youth Bureau
17/23 Albion Street, Leicester LE16GD.

Scottish Community Education Centre
Atholl House, 2 Canning Street, Edinburgh EH38EG.

The Richmond Fellowship
8 Addison Road, London W148DL.
(Runs therapeutic centres for those suffering from mental and nervous breakdowns.)

Young Men's Christian Association
National Personnel Department, 640 Forest Road, London E173DZ.

B.Ed, B.A, Cert.Ed, Et al...

So far we have considered teachers as if they were a homogenous group, but as far as the labour market is concerned the different routes taken into teaching may present different problems and different opportunities. This section focuses on some of these distinctions.

The section begins by considering the rating given by employers outside the broad educational field to the teaching certificate as such and suggests areas of work which those teachers who do not possess a degree might consider. It goes on to view the BEd as a degree, rather than as a professional qualification, in terms of its market value to employers, and then considers the position of the newly-qualified graduate with a Postgraduate Certificate of Education (PGCE). The final sub-section deals with the possibilities of enhancing a qualification.

Back to 'O' Levels
Although the three-year certificate route into the teaching profession has now been phased out, there will still be many young and comparatively inexperienced teachers with this qualification, and there are, of course, very many highly experienced teachers who may be interested in the 'market value' of the teaching qualification as such. Statistically, over recent years, the newly qualified without a degree fared worse in obtaining a first teaching post, though the figures would have been influenced by the higher proportion of certificated teachers training for primary work than in the graduate

population, at a time when the primary sector was hardest hit by the falling school rolls. It therefore seems still important to spare some space to consider this as well as degree qualifications in relation to the employment market. The last intake to the present 3-year diploma course will be in session 1983/84 and the first intake to the new 4-year degree course will not take place until the 1984/85 academic session, which means that graduates from that course will not appear until the summer of 1988. There will therefore be no conflict for jobs between the two groups. The last output of diplomates will have two years before the first of the new graduates enter the job market and those already in mid course will have correspondingly longer to establish themselves in the teaching profession. For many years to come, teachers who have qualified by the diploma route will outnumber their colleagues qualifying by the new degree route and there is no reason to expect that their career prospects will be adversely affected.

Some of the jobs for which a teaching qualification may be highly regarded have been discussed in Section Four. Apart from these and from some exceptions referred to below, the Teachers' Certificate in itself is not recognised as a qualification for any other profession. Its marketable value to an employer is rarely related to the actual course, only to whatever qualities it may have developed in its holder. In this latter respect it is rather like an arts degree, but a degree is now a recognised entry point to many training schemes; is a minimum qualification for quite a number of professions; gives exemption from specific parts of many examinations for professional qualifications or is the basic requirement for entry to the examination.

The experienced teacher will find his or her *experience* useful for many jobs and this aspect is dealt with in more detail in the sections which follow.

Both new and older teachers seeking a change of career are often disheartened to discover that employers, as far as qualifications are concerned, consider them in relation to their GCE/SCE qualifications rather than accepting what teachers naturally regard as the higher achievement. For many posts (e.g. in banks) specific 'O' level/grade passes (e.g. English and mathematics) are required, and sometimes requirements are rigidly adhered to. Having done mathematics within one's certificate may well not be considered an acceptable alternative to 'O' level/grade maths, whatever the standard of the certificate course. This can be because employers do not regard the certificate highly, possibly assuming it is entirely concerned with methodology and is therefore a non-relevant professional qualification. It may be because staff are expected to work for appropriate professional qualifications for which the 'O' level/grade passes are initial requirements. Whatever the reason, it can sound very depressing indeed, but the teacher may in reality be in no more disadvantageous a position than any graduate unable to find a suitable graduate training scheme place. Once the applicant has found a post, it is something of a blow to self-esteem to discover that he or she could have had a similar job with two 'A' levels or, worse still, five 'O' levels! But the idea of 'graduate status' jobs is, apart from a few professions such as medicine, relatively new. Many company directors did begin as office boys (bright ones — admittedly!)

An education isn't necessarily 'wasted' just because a *first* job consists of tasks which an intelligent school-leaver could perform. Such experience can be turned to good account. In my first job as a graduate trainee journalist all poised to write scintillating letters, theatre reviews and the book page, I at last got a couple of paragraphs in print (I think I cut them out and may indeed still have them somewhere). One was a follow-up of the morning paper's story of a local boy taken ill after eating poisonous berries — I did the hospital bulletin 'progressing satisfactorily'; the other was the weather. You didn't really need 'O' levels to do either! In a career the prospects and potential are more important than the *initial* level of work.

Here are a few of the possible alternative careers you might consider. (Consult the books listed in the bibliography for further suggestions and information.)

The *retail trade* is still recruiting and recruits quite a proportion of its future management personnel at the 'A' level/ 'H' grade plus stage. This is certainly an area where the personal qualities and skills which teaching develops are highly valued — viz. the ability to relate to people, communication skills, self-discipline, adapting to an organisation. If, in addition, you welcome the competitive atmosphere of retailing and are able to be mobile, especially during the training period, you are likely to be an attractive candidate. Before applying for any retail management scheme you should get some experience, perhaps as Saturday staff in a supermarket or during the sales and Christmas periods as a temp. This will not only help you decide yourself whether this world would attract you, but demonstrates to the personnel officer or staff manager who receives your application that you have some idea of what is involved. You can make a general application to the departmental stores or supermarket chains which appeal. You will find details of many organisations in the directories referred to on page 80.

Sometimes young teachers find out accidentally that retail management offers a worthwhile career. I have known several cases of young men and women taking a sales assistant job on a temporary basis because they could not get a teaching post, and enjoying it so much that they have been invited to join the management training scheme or have used the experience to apply successfully to another firm. Although retail management is a job that needs energy and commitment, people in their late twenties and early thirties should not be deterred from applying. One staff manageress told me that she had recently taken on a 34-year-old teacher who was proving a most successful trainee.

The *hotel and catering industry* is short of staff and is only just beginning to gear itself to the degree-level entrant. Don't think of this as simply a career for embryonic *Escoffiers*, but as one with considerable potential for those with perhaps less genius but a generous capacity for organisation and hard work. At the top end of the scale in institutional catering management you might land a post such as catering manager and adviser for a university.

Accountancy is an expanding profession, open at the moment to graduates and non-graduates. Don't restrict yourself just to considering chartered accountancy, and within chartered accountancy just to the big names. If you do you may find entry, particularly to the prestigious larger partnerships, is so competitive at the moment that effectively only graduates are considered. Find out about some of the other five accountancy bodies, such as Cost and Management or Certified. Enquiries can often be helped by centrally or regionally based careers advisers, who act on behalf of the professional organisation and offer advice and introductions. See Useful Addresses for the addresses of professional associations. Generally speaking, if you do not possess a degree you will need two 'A' levels/3 'A' grades and three 'O' levels/2 'O' grades (including maths and English) but individual accountancy bodies will tell you the precise requirements.

Work Study is a wide ranging career which appreciates higher education combined with industrial experience.

There are many other careers to which your 'O' and 'A' level/'O' and 'H' grades qualifications may gain you entry and for which you can train on the job. For example: *insurance, estate agency work, nursing, legal executive.*

The *Civil Service* is still recruiting, though competition is stiff. The Executive Officer Grade (minimum two 'A' levels/ 3 'H' grades) is currently holding exams at fixed points in the year rather than running a continuous recruitment scheme. You will find good honours graduates competing at this level along with school-leavers. If you are successful, however, the Civil Service offers a wide variety of work and utilises many talents and different kinds of expertise, from the statistician to the librarian, the linguist to the archaeologist. The Civil Service publishes a series of most useful guides to a wide range of careers in the public service, including one for those with GCE/SCE qualifications. These pamphlets are available in careers offices.

Those who were attracted to teaching partly because they like the idea of working in the public service may also be attracted to *local government.* Like the Civil Service it has a wide range of functions, some of which, like recreation provision, are discussed elsewhere. It administers the education and library services, housing and so on. Like any business it also supports these services with departments dealing with accounts and supplies and personnel. Many staff enter on the basis of 'O' and 'A' levels/'O' and 'H' grades and staff are encouraged to work part-time for appropriate professional qualifications. If you are ambitious you will probably have to be prepared to relocate in order to get promotion. (BEd students should note that some local authorities run graduate training schemes and you should contact your institution's careers service for details of these.) You could enquire about opportunities through the personnel department of your authority. Clerical level posts may be advertised in the local press. *Opportunities* is the professional paper, and consists almost entirely of advertisements for staff. It is not available from newsagents but should be in the public library. Most posts require some experience, but it does also contain traineeships. Some posts, especially senior ones, are advertised in the national press. If you are seriously interested in this work, you should certainly spend some time studying back copies of *Opportunities,* since advertisements are often very specific about requirements and detailed in describing the jobs.

One skill area for which short intensive courses are available is *secretarial* work. Highly experienced secretaries in London can now command salaries of £6,000-£8,000 but good shorthand and typing speeds, as well as such personal qualities as tact and initiative, are important for posts at this level which at the top end of the scale are PA jobs. One of the attractions of secretarial work is the variety of environments in which the work can be carried out, from publishing companies to art galleries, hospitals to export companies.

Among some interesting secretarial posts offered in 1981/2 within the arts field were: assistant secretary to a music publisher ('knowledge of classical and contemporary music desirable' £4,500); secretary/PA to a publisher (basically secretarial but 'some editorial work, languages a distinct advantage. Salary according to experience.'); and secretaries in the drama department of the Arts Council (starting between £4,992 and £5,267 on scale to £6,118). If you are interested in the arts administration field itself, you should consult Section Seven.

Among some of the less run-of-the-mill jobs on offer in one issue of the *Daily Telegraph* were a personal assistant to a probation officer, a legal secretary and information officer for a professional association - and it is still true that many women in executive positions in industry began as secretaries.

If You Have a BEd
Until very recently a BEd was thought of as a professional qualification for teaching rather than a degree, but it is worth considering the value of your BEd in the latter light. After all, many people with law degrees don't become solicitors and barristers, and quite a number of people with degrees in medicine go into industry or commerce.

Your BEd will not guarantee you a job, of course, and you may find some employers regard it in a less favourable light than a BA. You would be wise to make it clear in your applications and at any interviews, which disciplines your degree covered. (For example, you might stress that you studied French in a strongly language-based course and that your education studies involved a special option in psychology, or sociology.) Some employers still think that only teaching method is studied in any depth in an education degree!

In large organisations it can even happen that, though the head office recognises the BEd as an 'any discipline' degree for recruitment purposes, the information has not yet filtered down to branch level. Nevertheless, careers advisers in colleges and polytechnics and BEd graduates themselves have done much to alert employers to the value of this degree. In the last year or so, BEd graduates have sucessfully entered as graduate trainees a wide range of careers, from retailing to industrial management to computer programming.

No degree — not even an Oxford first — guarantees you a job, but a degree puts you in the running for a number of careers or gives you a substantial advantage. The entry to some professions is in name, and to many more in practice, graduate-only. It is increasingly the pattern for professions to move to graduate-only status.

Solicitors are among the professional people seriously moving in this direction. Accountancy is a profession where this is being debated and, from January 1981, all entrants to librarianship follow either a professional degree course at a library school or a postgraduate course.

Some professional examinations can only be taken by graduates (or equivalents). Many industrial and commercial firms have a graduate level entry scheme. Large organisations or national bodies may have a graduate entry point which is either the only opening to senior posts or offers the greatest promise of promotion.

With a degree you are, for example, eligible for the Army Education Corps, or for the graduate accelerated promotion entry of the police, or for the Administrative Grade of the Civil Service which covers a very wide range of work indeed. Among the opportunities are the following: inspectors of factories; prison governors; map research officers; museum research assistants and administrators. You are also, provided you are under 35 years of age (30 in Scotland), eligible for the Health Service Administration 27-month training scheme. You need to be mobile during the training period. Apply to the personnel officer of your own regional health authority. Staff can study part-time for the appropriate professional qualification (e.g. in supplies, personnel, finance or management services).

Occasionally, your training as a teacher is publicly acknowledged by potential employers. One life assurance firm, advertising for trainees in finance and sales within its marketing division, stipulated 'Graduate — any discipline. Lively personality. Numeracy and teacher training are advantages.' Somebody somewhere knows your worth!

It is worth noting that some firms and other organisations stipulate an honours degree for their graduate schemes.

If you hanker after a post in highly competitive fields like conservation or museum work you may find a degree is a great asset because, although there are jobs at 'A' level/'H' grade entry, in practice, all the people with any responsible work are graduates (or have equivalent professional qualifications). Many of the graduates will have higher degrees or relevant diplomas too!

In the Nature Conservancy Board, for example, apart from the Wardens' jobs, the few posts are entirely filled by graduates, usually with research degrees. In the museums, however, posts at junior levels (e.g. Curator Grade G) are advertised (e.g. in *The Daily Telegraph*, *The Evening Standard* for London museums, and *New Scientist*) from time to time). Assistants recruited at this level do have opportunities for promotion, but it is worth remembering that progress may well depend on further qualifications such as the Associateship of the Museums Association, and the Museums Association itself warns applicants that 'many posts in the museum world are open only to graduates and the preference for graduates is increasing'.

If you are considering using your degree for a career other than teaching but are unsure of the possibilities open to you, one of the most helpful starting points is the Careers Research and Advisory Centre (CRAC) publication *Graduate Employment and Training* (GET). It will give you information on the careers open to you on the basis of your degree; the number and type of vacancies that firms and public bodies are likely to have this year, and on the professional qualifications you may need to obtain in the career of your choice. The graduate recruiters' directories *GO, GET* and *DOG* (see bibliography for details) will give you information about other firms actively recruiting graduates.

Students sometimes wonder which of the categories of 'Subject of Degree' the BEd would be classified under. Broadly speaking, for the purpose of employment it falls under the 'Arts' or 'Any Discipline'. If, however, a major part of your course has been in a subject such as history, English or French, you could also consider jobs where these disciplines are sought. Many arts graduates these days take more than one area in their degree course and your course is very likely to have included just as many hours of study of English as some of these degree courses do. Point out, too, to prospective employers any specific and relevant features of your course. For example, an employer specifying that 'languages' is a useful subject to have taken may well be interested to know that your course emphasised communication in the spoken language rather than the study of literature. Directories such as *GO* and *DOG* are so arranged that it is comparatively easy to discover which employers are recruiting 'Arts' or 'Any Discipline' graduates. Your institution's careers advisory service should be able to give you a copy (or lend one) of the Association of Graduate Careers Advisory Services (AGCAS) information sheet called *Careers for Graduates of Any Subject* which may give you other ideas still.

Postgraduates
Much of what has been written above applies to postgraduates but there are one or two particular points worth making.

Graduates on a one-year course have made their decision to teach very recently, and to be faced with the possibility of having to change direction so rapidly may be quite frightening. If you are among this group, it may be of some consolation to know that your reactions are not unique. I have been surprised how many of the graduates I have discussed this with over the last few years have never considered any other job, except perhaps advertising or the BBC in their more rosy-coloured moments. Only when the prospect of being unemployed looms ahead do they seriously think 'What do I want from my work?' and 'What have I to offer other than my subject?' Some who drifted into teaching find this gives them a chance to reassess their aims. For the first time they may ask themselves questions like 'What actually goes on in industry?' and may find the answers more interesting and attractive than they expected.

If you did make a very careful and deliberate choice of teaching as a career, you will take comfort from the knowledge that over the last few years the vast majority of postgraduates who wanted to teach got teaching jobs. A substantial number of those who failed to do so were married women seeking posts in a restricted geographical area.

To people in this position who are determined to teach, one can only emphasize that if circumstances force you to be inflexible on one count, you must be as flexible as possible on others, e.g. age-range of pupils, teaching subject and type of school.

Postgraduates considering other careers are probably best advised to go for something where training can be done on the job, since a further grant for vocational training (on a discretionary basis) may well *not* be forthcoming.

Enhancing Your Qualifications
Although practical experience is often much more important than paper qualifications in determining who gets the job, there is no doubt that there are times when that 'little bit of paper' matters, whether you are looking for a change of career, or for promotion within your own field. Often, too, even where the actual qualification is of no great market value, the learning process you went through to get it helps you advance your career, though not always in the direction you anticipated when you embarked on the course. Study, like travel, broadens the mind — and your horizons.

In England and Wales, the serving teacher with a certificate may well be able to study part-time or full-time for an in-service BEd at a nearby college of higher education or polytechnic. In Scotland it is planned that within the next few years part-time degree courses will become available in most, if not all, of the colleges of education. These courses will be intended specifically for practising teachers. The overall number of places to be provided on these courses has not yet been finally fixed and will to some extent be determined in the light of demand. For further information regarding in-service training write to the Scottish Education Department, 43 Jeffrey Street, Edinburgh EH1 1DN. The National Association of Teachers in Further and Higher Education (NATFHE) Handbook (see bibliography) has a list of BEd courses available for serving teachers with, normally, at least two years' experience. Teachers can apply to their employing authorities for grant aid. A BEd degree can be gained in one year (hons, two years) full-time at some institutions.

Another possibility is to take an Open University degree, for which teachers may be granted advanced standing, enabling them to complete the degree with fewer units. There is an account of the University in *Second Chances 1983* and much information is available from the University itself. Advantages are the wide choice of courses, the possibility of working at your own pace; disadvantages — the cost (if you don't get grant aid) and the fact that distance learning does not suit everyone.

There is a very wide range of advanced diplomas and masters' degrees available on both part-time and full-time bases at universities, polytechnics and colleges throughout the country. Some of these have a highly specific vocational slant, e.g. in educational administration, the teaching of the handicapped, or counselling. Others, though certainly relevant to the classroom — curriculum development, for instance — less obviously lead in a particular career direction.

Some masters' degrees are professional in that they have pedagogical concerns. This is true of all MEds, but also of some MAs. Other masters' degrees may be appropriate professionally to the secondary school teacher or higher education lecturer, but are primarily subject-orientated (e.g. MA in Victorian Literature).

What Do They Involve?
The nomenclature of advanced diplomas and higher degrees is confusing to the uninitiated. Although the term 'diploma' has a more serious and academic ring to it, it is used interchangeably with 'certificate' for many purposes, but some institutions, on the other hand, do distinguish between the words and 'diploma' is then usually the more advanced award. Diploma and certificate courses are taught courses which will demand attendance at fixed lecture times and often involve periods of practical work too.

Masters' degrees lasting for one year full-time (or the part-time equivalent) are normally taught courses, though there is often the opportunity to present a dissertation on some appropriate topic of one's choice. This opportunity is also available within some diploma courses. Some institutions use the term Master of Philosophy (MPhil) to distinguish higher degrees obtained entirely by research, but others use the terms MA and MSc for both taught and research degrees. Working for a higher degree by research alone is an attractive proposition for the part-time student *if* he or she has a suitable subject to hand, good access to appropriate sources, well-disciplined study habits, and is able to sustain interest over many months with possibly minimal supervision and little or no group support. For very many teachers the taught course is probably a more sensible choice, especially if they have been out of the habit of sustained study for some years. In any case, it may well be possible to develop a dissertation subject into an MA or even a PhD if you get the urge for study.

Will You Be Eligible?
There is no straightforward answer to this, and if you find a course which really attracts you, you should always enquire about it from the relevant department, even if you are not sure whether you meet the normal entry requirements. Entry regulations usually include the word 'normally' and you might be just the sort of exception envisaged when they put that important word in! Or the staff may be able to suggest a lower-level course which could ultimately lead to the one you want.

Bearing that proviso in mind, the following remarks give general guidance. If a course is termed 'in-service', it probably means what it says and teachers should currently be teaching in a school — not necessarily a maintained school. There are, however, courses which are suitable for the returner.

Professional advanced certificates and diplomas usually require teaching experience of three years, sometimes longer. The same applies to professionally-orientated higher degrees, although there are some which are suitable for the newly qualified.

Taught masters' degrees ask for a first degree (sometimes an honours degree) in addition, although MEds will often occasionally accept a teaching certificate plus substantial experience, or initial training plus an advanced diploma in education. The subject-based MA or MSc will naturally not demand any professional experience, but will probably ask for an honours degree, possibly a 'good honours degree', in a relevant subject. If you want to do the degree by research, you will almost certainly need a good honours degree, again in the relevant subject.

Will You Get a Grant?
Again, there is no straightforward answer to this one. In England and Wales some authorities will second teachers on full-time courses, or give some financial support for part-time ones. Some courses carry a certain number of state bursaries and for others it may be possible to apply to the DES for a state grant. In practice, to qualify for these bursaries you need a first-class or top-second degree, and there are age limits too (e.g. normally, under 40 for state bursaries for professional and vocational courses, and under 35 for the studentships for full-time study and research). In Scotland apply to Scottish Education Department, Awards Branch, Haymarket House, Edinburgh EH1 1DN.

The directories mentioned below and, of course, individual prospectuses will give some information on whether grants are available.

Where Can You Find Out?
· Professionally relevant in-service courses for England and Wales are listed in the DES *Programme of Long Courses for Teachers*. The National Committee for the In-Service Training of Teachers organise national courses and other courses of interest for the in-service training of teachers and others engaged in the educational service in Scotland. Further information from Scottish Education Department, 43 Jeffrey Street, Edinburgh EH1 1DN. Postgraduate qualifications of all kinds are listed in *Graduate Studies*. BEd courses are listed in the NATFHE Handbook. It is always worth contacting your local higher education institution to see what is available — or likely to become available in the next year or so — locally. Sources of finance for the older student are discussed in *Second Chances 1983*. (See bibliography for details.)

Useful Addresses

Association of Certified Accountants
Student Services Department, 29 Lincoln's Inn Fields, London WC2A 3EE.

Banking Information Service
10 Lombard Street, London EC3V 9AR.

Institute of Bankers in Scotland
20, Rutland Square, Edinburgh EH1 2BB.

Chartered Institute of Public Finance and Accountancy
The Education and Training Officer, 1 Buckingham Place, London SW1E 6HS.

Institute of Chartered Accountants
Chartered Accountants Hall, PO Box 433, Moorgate Place, London EC2P 2BJ.

Institute of Chartered Accountants of Scotland
27 Queen Street, Edinburgh EH2 1LA.

Institute of Cost and Management Accountants
Education Department, 63 Portland Place, London W1N 4AB.

Institute of Cost and Management Accountants
Scottish Education Officer, Manse Road, Milnathort, Kinross, Perthshire.

Nursing and Health Service Careers Centre
121/3 Edgware Road, London W2 2HX.

The Library Association
7 Ridgmount Street, London WC1E 7AE.
(information on librarianship and training courses)

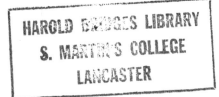

THE OLDER TEACHER AND THE RETURNER

WELCOME BACK MR CHIPS

This section discusses some general questions of importance to experienced teachers considering a change of career, to those facing redundancy, to would-be returners and to newly-qualified mature graduates.

It first considers opportunities for retraining. It then looks at possibilities for career change and the attitudes of employers towards the older applicant, and offers some advice to particular groups of older teachers. Although reference is made here to various specific careers by way of example, the main discussion of possible new careers, for which teaching experience is valuable, is in Section Seven. Many of the suggestions made in earlier sections are also applicable.

Retraining
One year retraining schemes are available in England and Wales for those intending to teach shortage subjects in secondary schools, viz. maths, physical sciences, craft and technology and business studies. If you are a qualified teacher over 28 and have not taken a full-time course of higher or further education in the previous five years, you are eligible, if accepted on a course, for the special scheme of government finance. This scheme covers those who wish to re-enter the profession and serving teachers not employed by local authorities. Other serving teachers may be able to get LEA secondment.

53

The DES gives brief details of the scheme and a list of colleges offering courses in its various leaflets (see Useful Addresses). The relevant ones are *Training and Retraining to Teach, Teaching the Physical Sciences and Mathematics, Teaching Business Studies in Secondary Schools* and *Teaching Craft, Design and Technology.* The individual colleges offering the courses produce information sheets or short prospectuses and usually you will find someone in the department happy to discuss the course informally with you, if you are seriously interested. Whilst their aims are the same, the contents of courses may vary, and so may the initial qualifications required. For example, one college expects 'A' level maths (or its equivalent) for its mathematics course, whereas another says that, whilst it particularly seeks those with an 'A' level in maths, it will consider those with a good 'O' level and evidence of further mathematical study. Business study retraining courses will probably expect subjects such as English and maths at 'O' level, and the courses should enable you to reach the appropriate level in skill subjects like shorthand and typing by the end of the course.

Although all these subjects are, at the time of writing, regarded as 'shortage' the position *may* have changed in some localities by the time you read this book. *Particularly if you are likely to be restricted to one geographical area*, you should check with the LEA as to the expected vacancy position at the end of your course.

Informed opinion suggests that whatever happens, in the foreseeable future there will still be a shortage of specialist mathematics, physics and chemistry teachers, especially since people with expertise in these areas are needed in the primary as well as the secondary sector.

It is even possible that there may be, in the not too distant future, courses for teachers to retrain as primary staff, since some optimists (or pessimists, depending on how you look at it) predict a shortfall of available primary teachers resultant on the cut-backs in training of recent years, and the rising birth-rate.

Career Change
Since first writing this book, I have had many contacts — both personal and by letter — with experienced teachers seeking advice on a change of career. Although individuals may sometimes present sets of circumstances and preferences which are quite difficult to reconcile, there is one sense in which it is much easier to discuss the whole question of career change with an individual rather than writing for the unknown reader; with an individual you do know what the starting point is! With the general reader in mind the possibilities are infinitely varied.

In the abstract, there are many opportunities open to the older teacher looking for a change. In practice, for some individuals the limiting factors of experience, age and personal circumstances may mean realistic possibilities are few. (This doesn't, incidentally, apply just to teachers. A recent analysis of the supply and demand for engineers makes much the same point about specialist experience within engineering. For others what looks at first sight a restricted picture proves, when past experience and other skills and talents are examined, to be one with many opportunities. The best advice I can give to the 'unknown reader', the experienced teacher considering career change, is to think hard about all the factors which I shall discuss in this section, in relation to himself or herself, and to read through the many suggestions in the rest of the book with as open a mind as possible, and then to follow some of them up by the appropriate specific enquiries or job searches. Don't just leave it at the 'thinking about it' stage.

I emphasise this because it is my experience that a very common failing — at any age — is to 'turn down' jobs which appear in many ways attractive, before filling in the application form, in some cases, before even discovering what the job really involves, and then subsequently to waste energy and effort worrying about lost opportunities. Put like that it sounds absurd, yet that effectively is what many of us do. We are so anxious not to make a mistake, not to take too big a risk, perhaps fearful of being rejected, that we mentally block out all sorts of interesting possibilities without giving them any serious consideration. Remember that asking for information about a post doesn't mean you've accepted it. You can only commit yourself when you are actually offered it.

Should you find yourself hastily turning over the pages and dismissing every suggestion with excuses — 'Oh, I can't see myself doing that.' 'It's very competitive, they won't look at me.' 'Perhaps it may not pay enough.' — ask yourself if you seriously want a change at all. Possibly you just want to be reminded that for you a switch would mean too much hassle, and the job you have suits you as well as any. On the other hand, you may genuinely want, or be forced, to make a change but were rather hoping for an easier solution to your problem than this book, or any other, can give. If that is the case, I suggest you make a serious start with your enquiries. Explore several avenues at once. It saves time in the long run and, in the course of your exploration, you will make contacts and pick up information (about training courses, possible useful temporary experience, etc.) that may well lead to a satisfying and possibly unexpected post. I have certainly known cases where someone applied for a job, although it was not ideal, but in the course of the interview heard about another one — and got it! Luck? Well, yes — but luck that depended on the person's willingness to create and respond to opportunities.

The posts open to you will depend upon a great many individual factors, your personal talents and skills, and your experience. Experience needs to be viewed in the widest sense; *all* the jobs you have ever held, the voluntary organisational tasks you have undertaken, child care, travel and so on.

Suppose you are a married woman with children of secondary school age. You doubt whether you will get a post teaching English again after a gap of some years. You can drive. You can type a little — you had to when you acted as the PTA secretary. For the past two years, you have been helping with an association for prisoners' wives. You see yourself as a calm and organised sort of person, not madly extrovert, but a good communicator. What might you consider? You first need to look carefully at your circumstances. Particular personal factors are set out in the sub-section on 'Potential Returners'. There are also financial considerations. Can you, for instance, afford to support yourself on a course if necessary? Would a part-time job offer adequate remuneration? And there are the considerations of the employment market. This varies quite dramatically according to location, and in some jobs could be radically affected by your age. (See below.)

Even if you confine yourself to 'experience-related' work, there are several possibilities which would seem certainly well worth exploring: retraining for business studies; teaching in further education; probation work; social work; work as an education welfare officer; charity administration, perhaps initially in a modest or part-time capacity.

On the other hand, a man in his late twenties, currently teaching PE and spending a good deal of his leisure time on outdoor activities, might look initially at recreation management in both private and public sectors. His physical fitness, allied to other qualities, might lead him to consider the police force — even the fire service. His extrovert personality and stamina might make him think about sales.

Leisure pursuits themselves occasionally lead to a complete change — like the primary school deputy head with a passion for fell-walking. He became a country park ranger. Or a casual opportunity may initiate change. The director of one large holiday company told me that he knew of several teachers who, having used his organisation's facilities for the school parties they accompanied, took up new careers in the holiday and tourist trade, both with his own company and with others.

If you are a practising teacher and decide to make a complete switch of career, you need to be aware that initially you nay well not get a better salary, perhaps not even a comparable one. A lower salary is most likely where complete retraining is necessary and you are regarded as a beginner, or where the career itself is, on average, less well paid than teaching. Some teachers, like the country ranger, regard this as an acceptable 'trade-in' for what they regard as a more satisfying way of life. Others hope to recoup the loss once they have experience in their new jobs. Where the teaching experience in itself is relevant (see Section Seven) the new post may, of course, offer an enhanced salary right from the start. For instance, a teacher who is head of a department is not going to have an easy move into personnel work at a better salary just because he or she fancies a change. Well-paid jobs in personnel demand experience. The teacher might, however, move into personnel work in local government via another administrative job, say in the education department, where teaching experience is valuable. Or the move might first be into industrial training in the FE sector, and through this into personnel work in industry, where the training experience is seen as highly relevant. In both these cases the new career will draw on the previous experience, and it would certainly not be unreasonable to expect to make the sideways move at an attractive level of salary. But the teacher who wrote to a professional institute, saying he would like to break into personnel work as he felt there were no prospects in teaching, *but* he'd need a salary of at least £10,000 initially — what should he do? — was bound to get a disappointing answer.

How Will Employers View You?
Obviously, all that has been said before on the subject of the BEd still applies to you, the experienced teacher, but in addition you are both older and more experienced.

Will your age affect you adversely? It depends — on the age, and the job. Some professions, especially those with a welfare role, pastoral slant to them, demand maturity which means that older people have a positive advantage. Other jobs seem to demand youth. Advertising, for example, is a very young profession. Over 25 you will find it very difficult to break in. As a general guide — all the evidence suggests that, providing you have the relevant basic qualifications and necessary commitment for the new career, up to the age of 25 or so, employers will accept your switch of job as quite normal. They will probably have taken on others of your age, and you won't present too many problems for their pension scheme and salary structure. Up to the age of 30 there are still very many professions which it is possible to enter with relatively little difficulty. After that age you may well find problems in trying to enter certain jobs. Even where, for example in accountancy, it is perfectly acceptable to the professional bodies that you become a student and sit the examinations, you may have to persevere to obtain a trainee post.

There is rarely a straightforward answer such as, 'At 32 you are too old.' Let us consider one example in some detail. The computer industry is a young one and, particularly in some small computer houses, you may well find objections on the grounds that you would be older than senior staff! The industry is just not geared to take mature people as beginners. When, at a conference, I asked delegates from computer software houses what their attitude to applications from women graduates of 30 plus would be, they seemed to be surprised to hear that there *were* women coming on to the labour market at that age and looking for a new career. But they did say that they would consider them if they were highly committed. At the time of writing, the shortage in the computer field is of experienced staff rather than the new entrant, so you would have to be persistent. Clearly, if you are currently working in school, it would be sensible to get as much computer experience as you can through your present job, and to look first for posts where you can claim your overall experience might be useful — in training or sales functions, for example. And there are always exceptions. It was a British consultancy in computing that sought interested BEd graduates, who had had an element of computer studies in their degree, to train as technical writers. 'Mature students welcome,' the recruiter said. 'Even up to 50 years old.' But then he'd been trained as a teacher himself!

Over 40 the career changer may well find severe restrictions, and the best course might well prove to be a search for work for which one's teaching experience is recognised as valuable, if not essential; the kind of work discussed in the next section.

Whatever your age there are some general points you should bear in mind. Never allow yourself to be put off by a few rejections which you assume to be on grounds of age. (There may be other reasons why you were rejected. These employers may be atypical.) Keep on trying. Some employers have general prejudices based on age — 'Awkward for the salary structure', 'Older people are inflexible', 'They will expect too much money', 'They won't fit in with younger people' — but a well-argued case can often dispel these fears. Your application, without in any way suggesting possible objections, can deal with them in a positive way by providing evidence that counters possible arguments against you on the grounds of age. Not 'Although I am forty, I consider myself still flexible etc.', but 'In my present post, as one of a relatively young team, I have had to deal with both x and y', and in the paragraph dealing with your leisure pursuits, you could include something which you have taken up fairly recently and in which you have achieved some considerable success. Whatever the job there are always exceptions that prove the rule - and *enough exceptions change the rule.*

Plenty of employers testify to the value of their 'older recruits'. One educational publisher told me his best salesman came to him in his mid-thirties, and elsewhere in this book, you will find other examples (e.g. Section Five, page 45). Different firms within the same industry have different policies, so it is worth persisting.

Many jobs in the private sector are never advertised and speculative letters, accompanied by a good curriculum vitae, are a particularly appropriate job-search method for the experienced person. Some of the books listed in the bibliography cover this aspect in some detail.

Although many public services have age limits for entry, they may be much higher than you imagine. The limit for executive officer in the Civil Service is now 45 years. For social work courses some institutions specify a *minimum* age of 25 or 30. Where maximum ages are stated, they can be as high as 50. Similar courses, which train probation officers and stipulate maximum ages, put them as high as 45 or 50.

Mature Students
Mature students have often made considerable sacrifices to return to college, and the

adjustment to the possibility of unemployment at the end may be uncomfortable. My own experience is that mature students cope extremely well — one of the advantages of 'maturity'! They may have a previous career to fall back on or this may help them get a teaching job. One married woman, restricted to a limited geographical area, landed a secondary English post — in short supply in her part of the world! — because she could also contribute to the commercial department on the basis of her previous career as a secretary. The further education lecturer mentioned on page 15 (Section Two) is another example. If they are married women, they may be able to stand a period of unemployment, and be the only available person in the area when a teaching job comes up on a temporary or part-time basis, or at an awkward time of the year at short notice. If they do manage to get an interview they often get the job. (Their maturity must be reassuring to selection panels.)

In making applications and preparing for interviews, it may boost your confidence to remember one or two points. In addition to your previous experience (paid, voluntary and domestic) you have just proved by successfully taking a higher education course that you can:
— adjust to a new organisation
— cope with completely new work schedules
— manage a full-time and demanding occupation as well as your domestic commitments.
A number of books in the bibliography are directed at the older career changer, some specifically at married women. I can particularly recommend *Career Change*.

Potential Returners
There is a large pool of married women who are trained teachers and who left the profession to bring up their families and who may well have intended to return to teaching in due course. In England and Wales the DES recognises them in its calculations, the colloquially and somewhat unflatteringly named PIT (pool of inactive teachers).

Over the next few years there may well be a demand for the primary-trained teacher and the PIT will no doubt provide many of them. But there are other married women teachers who may well hope for a change of direction. If you are one of these you will need to consider carefully a number of points. Is your priority money, or a new interest in life? Is domestic convenience of paramount importance to you? If so, you might consider a part-time job or job-sharing.

Job-sharing on any scale is a comparatively recent concept, a formalisation of what many part-time jobs have amounted to in the past. It means simply that one job is split between two people; the work being split in different ways, either by time (such as mornings and afternoons, or one week on / one week off) or by function. Although Barclays Bank has been running such a scheme since the early 1940s, the idea is still regarded as new (and with some suspicion) by many employers and employees. In recent months, however, I have noticed quite a number of advertisements mentioning 'job-sharing' as a possibility. The Equal Opportunities Commission has produced a study of the subject called *Job-Sharing - Improving the quality and availability of part-time work*. New Ways to Work publishes two booklets *Job Sharing - A Guide for Employees* price 60p and *Job Sharing - A Guide for Employees* price 75p. Prices include postage and packing. They tell you how to go about looking for a job-sharing post and how to present the arguments in favour of the scheme to employers (showing that it will cost the employer no more or involve only marginally higher administrative costs, that it has benefits in terms of potential holiday relief, etc, etc.).

I have never formally job-shared, but I did work as a part-time teacher for five years in a school which successfully employed a number of part-timers. I can testify that two half-timers willingly give more in enthusiasm and energy than one full-time worker can possibly muster. (We all seemed to run extra-curricular activities on a similar level to the full-timers!) On the other hand, the limited responsibility and hours at work are a great relief if one is juggling with both a career and domestic responsibilities. ·

Some women who think of returning to work after a number of years are worried about being 'rusty' — even in jobs they have done before. In considering a change of career they can lack confidence more acutely. It is important to develop self-confidence and there are a number of ways in which you can do this. Taking on a fairly responsible job in a voluntary organisation can be a useful way back to the world of work. For some reason many people find this type of responsibility less threatening than the same level of responsibility for which they are paid. Or taking a course may be the answer. You may be eligible for a TOPS grant for certain courses. *Second Chances 1983* covers the broad range of state and private provision in adult education including correspondence courses. To find out about whether you, and the course which interests you, are likely to attract TOPS finance, you should contact the Jobcentre.

For many women a part-time, temporary or fairly undemanding job may be what they want initially on returning to employment.

Redundant Teachers

Should you have been made redundant, you ought first to make use of all the possible sources of help, from the advisory services described in Section Two to some of the books directed at the redundant executive. Your employer may offer the opportunity for vocational counselling, help with job-search strategies, etc., and it sometimes happens that the quite natural resentment against the employer causes people to refuse this disdainfully. The gesture possibly gives a psychological fillip at the time, but is not really to be recommended. Even if you think you have another job all sewn up and waiting in the wings, take the support offered. You never know what may come of it.

Most of the books directed at those who are redundant (or suspect they might be heading that way) choose their examples largely from commerce and industry, but the general advice they offer is still applicable — covering subjects such as financial reorganisation, job-search strategies, discussion to help you understand your own reactions to what is certainly, for most people, a traumatic experience.

It may be a number of years since you took your degree or certificate, but it is still possible that your university or college careers advisory service may be able to offer some help. At the very least, most would offer you the facilities of their information room. You may very well be able to get access to vacancy information. It may even be possible to have an advisory interview. The pressures on these services from current students have increased considerably in recent months, and this at a time of cuts — in some cases in both manpower and resources — obviously affects the amount of assistance which can be given to former students. Those who graduated a certain number of years ago may be asked to pay a charge for these services at some institutions. Despite these staffing difficulties, careers advisers generally are by nature inclined to be helpful. At the least you will probably be directed to some useful source of advice or information.

If you have been unemployed for some considerable time, you may be eligible for a CP post, and for this reason alone it is worth contacting PER since these are included in *Executive Post*.

If you decide to retrain, you may be eligible for a Training Opportunities Programme (TOPS) grant if the course is regarded as appropriate, though some people who have successfully obtained TOPS finance have sometimes had to be pretty persistent to get it!

The age at which your redundancy occurs is obviously an important factor in determining the type of work available to you. If you are in your fifties the number of 'new' careers open to you is limited, but you may well be able to afford financially to look at some of the interesting but less well paid jobs, e.g. in charities, or perhaps even in part-time work, say in further education.

Useful Addresses

DES, The Information Division
Room 2/4 DES, Elizabeth House, York Road, London SE1 7TH.
(for information on retraining)

SED
43 Jeffrey Street, Edinburgh EH1 1DN.
(for information on pre-service and in service training)

Equal Opportunities Commission
Overseas House, Quay Street, Manchester M3 3HN.

Equal Opportunities Commission
249 West George Street, Glasgow.

New Ways to Work
347a Upper Street, London N1 0PD

SWITCHING TO A NEW FIELD

This section considers in more detail a number of careers for which experience of teaching is either a prerequisite or of value and relevance. Although this may not be immediately appropriate for the newly-qualified teacher, when embarking on a career it is always useful to know the chances of branching into other areas. There is a sub-section which offers an introduction to the possibility of self-employment.

Finally this survey is intended to alert those who are thinking about teaching as a career to opportunities. Knowing about such possibilities, may well prevent someone horrified at the prospect of 40 years before the blackboard (or perhaps the audio-visual aids), from abandoning the idea of teaching before even beginning! Once a teacher has a few years' good experience there are a number of interesting possibilities open to him or her. Some of these opportunities need a degree, others a particular kind of expertise, perhaps in age-range, ability level of pupils, experience obtained through extra-curricular work and so forth.

Married women who taught for a while, left to have a family and had hoped to return, but now find teaching posts scarce, may find some of the suggestions appropriate, particularly if they are in a position to embark on further training or re-training. The wide range of training courses cannot be dealt with here for reasons of space and you should consult a specialised guide such as *Second Chances for Adults* which explains in some detail adult education and training provision. If what you want is simply to check where you can train as a careers officer, or a journalist, or study antique furniture restoration, then you should consult directories (which list courses according to subject or career) such as *British Qualifications* or *Graduate Studies* or the *Directory of Further Education*. Details of all these books will be found in the bibliography.

An area of work which perhaps college students are likely to bear in mind is lecturing in teacher education! The recent further contraction of the colleges and sharp reduction in the number of initial teacher training places mean that opportunities in this field are likely to be very restricted for some time to come. Taking a long-term view, however, there are openings for teachers with good practical experience and appropriate higher degree or diplomas as lecturers for BEd, postgraduate and in-service teachers' courses offered in colleges, polytechnics and universities.

Competition for such posts is at present very keen and the requirements for lecturers appointed to polytechnics and colleges of higher education are likely to be equivalent to those for parallel university posts.

Similarly there are posts for advisers both with local authorities and with the inspectorate. There are also interesting opportunities working in teachers' centres, and some teachers find a satisfying career in educational administration. The range of administrative functions and organisations is quite wide. Some posts are appropriate only for career administrators but there are others where some teaching experience, perhaps in a particular sphere, is useful. Executive and administrative personnel are employed by, for example, local authority education departments, examination boards for GCE/SCE and also commercial and other specialist areas, some educational trusts, registration and examination departments in colleges, universities and polytechnics, and organisations as diverse as the Council for National Academic Awards (CNAA) and the Universities Central Council on Admissions (UCCA).

All these posts are advertised in periodicals such as the *Times Educational Supplement* and *Times Higher Education Supplement*, and advertisements also appear from time to time in daily national newspapers. The 'tail-end' of *The Guardian* education page advertisements often includes such openings. Administrative appointments in the education departments of local authorities are advertised in *Opportunities* and the educational press. *Opportunities* is not available from newsagents but should be in your local library. Very often adverts are carried in the local press. If you know which authority you would like to work for, you could also contact their personnel department to enquire about possible vacancies. Many educational administrators in local authorities moved into this field after a year or two in schools. It has not been usual to move back into schools but there have been some recent instances of senior administrators moving to headships in schools.

Some teachers move into very specialised areas of education (following further training where appropriate), such as teaching the deaf or blind, teaching in the prison service and borstal institutions, art, drama or music therapy with the mentally handicapped or disturbed. Such experience leads some to retrain for social work.

Specialist courses for the teaching of the deaf or blind are listed in the DES *Programme of Long Courses for Teachers*. Schools for the blind generally appoint experienced teachers from 'normal' schools and, within three years of their appointment, the DES expects them to pass the Schoolteachers' Diploma of the College of

Teachers of the Blind. In Scotland the information given for the teaching of the Deaf (see above) applies here for the teaching of the blind. (See Useful Addresses.) Most teachers of the deaf will also have worked with hearing pupils first. There is a trend towards teaching physically handicapped, and where appropriate mentally handicapped, children in special units attached to ordinary schools. This does, of course, offer teachers the opportunity to give assistance with children who are handicapped, to have small groups of children working within their own classes for certain lessons or activities, and to develop their own awareness of the problems children with different handicaps encounter, and of their potential. One teacher I know, having taught in primary schools and been a hospital teacher, is now a teacher in a purpose-built unit for the handicapped attached to a first school. Only those working with children with auditory or visual handicaps *must* acquire an extra qualification.

Therapists use the creative arts to help in the treatment of the physically and mentally handicapped and disturbed, and may work in a variety of settings — in schools, hospitals and prisons, for instance. There has been in recent years increasing appreciation of the value of this work by the educational, social welfare and medical professions. There is considerable variation within regions of the use made of these specialists.

Music therapists should have a wide knowledge and a love of music. Full-time courses for music graduates are offered by the Guildhall School of Music and Drama and the Nordoff Music Therapy Centre. Some relevant experience, e.g. teaching, especially of the handicapped, is a usual prerequisite. Short courses run by the British Society for Music Therapy are suitable for teachers who are working in, say, a special school and using music therapy as part of their work. A number of new posts have been created over the last few years and therapists frequently work on a peripatetic basis.

The British Association of Art Therapists produces, among other publications, a leaflet on the association, the work of art therapists and training courses available (see Useful Addresses). Some art therapists work in schools, though the majority designated as art therapists are employed in hospitals, sometimes on a part-time basis which is paid at a sessional rate. Some therapists are employed by the Home Office, full-time in prisons, borstals, etc.

The profession is still in the process of establishing itself. Hospitals differ in what they require from art therapists in the way of qualifications. The Department of Health and Social Security (DHSS) states that the normal requirement is an art qualification following at least two years' post 'A' level/ 'H' grade study. The Association of Art Therapists expects for full membership — a graduate qualification in art or design plus two years' work as an art therapist or recognised training. It recommends that intending art therapists go first to art school. Notwithstanding this, there are people practising in this field on the basis of very varied qualifications — occupational therapists, teachers and psychologists, for example, as well as artists. Some vacancies occur in the association's newsletter and also in the press, e.g. *New Society, Times Educational Supplement* and *Time Out*.

The first part-time course in drama therapy was started as recently as 1977 but there are now organisations of drama therapy. (See Useful Addresses.) The British Association of Drama Therapy produces a journal and has a list of (mainly short) courses. Sesame, another organisation, collaborates in a long drama therapy course.

Educational psychologists working in the schools psychological services or child guidance clinics, in addition to teaching experience and a teaching qualification, have either a one-year (for holders of a first degree in psychology) or two-year (for holders of other degrees) educational psychology qualification.

Health education offers some openings for experienced teachers, especially those with qualifications in biology, home economics, or similarly related subjects. This is still a developing profession, and since the main employers are area health authorities and local authorities, career opportunities are dependent on levels of public expenditure.

It is a career that, in general, demands relevant professional experience as well as qualifications, and teaching is a highly appropriate experience to offer. One post for a dental health study sought a senior associate for a three-year post in the dissemination field. The study, based at a major university researched and developed dental health packages for pre-school children and adolescents. Since this particular post involved responsibility for national dissemination of the adolescent programme, it asked for 'experience in schools' and 'skills in negotiation'.

At the lower end of the scale, teaching expeierence is useful to offer if you apply for a trainee post as a health education officer. Since this work involves responsibility for, and organisation of health education activities, administrative skills are increasingly in demand. Trainee officers would normally be seconded on an appropriate course. The type and level of provision varies between areas. Posts may be advertised in the health, educational and national press, also (for some posts) in *Opportunities* , or enquiries can be made directly to an employing authority.

The Health Education Council produces helpful literature but is not a direct employer of health educators, nor does it operate a vacancy service.

Many teachers become increasingly interested in pastoral work as their career progresses, and may consider counselling. There are both short in-service and one-year courses. It would be over-optimistic to suggest that there are many counselling posts vacant at the moment, but they do exist — in schools, universities and other Higher Education (HE) institutions, and with other non-educational agencies. Agencies employing paid staff are listed in *A Directory of Voluntary Counselling and Allied Services*, published by the British Association for Counselling. Other teachers go into the careers advisory service as careers officers, though increasingly the service is trying to recruit personnel with industrial and commercial experience, for obvious reasons. (They don't want to give birth to another version of the old tag about those who can't teach...) This might be exactly where your unwilling service of six months in the local plastics factory and half a year as a waitress or waiter before you landed your first teaching job actually turns out to be your greatest asset!

Posts, including trainee posts, are advertised by local authorities in *Opportunities*, the general press and educational press, as appropriate. There are training courses for both graduates and non-graduates. Another possibility is to enter the careers office as an employment assistant (who deals mainly with placements) and hope to be seconded for training in due course. One young teacher, now a specialist careers officer for the unemployed, was unable to obtain a teaching post and worked for a year as a local authority gardener. The combination of this experience plus his teaching qualification got him an employment assistant post, followed by secondment to a postgraduate Diploma in Vocational Guidance. Although many new careers officers are in their early twenties, this is a career where older recruits with several years of working experience are welcomed. A booklet about the work of the careers officer is published by the Local Government Training Board in co-operation with the Institute of Careers Officers. (See Useful Addresses.) The bulk of the careers officer's work is with the 16-19 year old age-group at the moment, with the main emphasis on the 16 year old school-leaver. However, if there should be a major shift in the direction of some kind of training place for all school-leavers, the nature of the careers officer's work, with its considerable emphasis on local and regional employment opportunities for the youngster, will change — quite in what direction is a subject for speculation.

Many professional bodies and trades organisations view training and career information as increasingly important functions. There has therefore been a small but significant increase in posts with such bodies where the post involves either a training consultancy function or a school or university liaison role. Such posts are advertised either in the appropriate professional journal or the national press.

Former teachers are also amongst those who go into industrial training and teaching in skill-centres. One voluntary organisation running workshops for the disabled told me that the full-time staff training the disabled to operate machinery and use workshop equipment had come from a variety of backgrounds. Some were themselves craftsmen and technicians. Others had been teachers. This organisation's workshops made a variety of products, including hand-decorated tiles and plates.

Charity administration itself does not directly relate to teaching, but it is a field which is suitable for the older entrant, and for some posts the ability to communicate well with groups of people, including children, is a prime requirement. Many of those who are employed by charities have had experience of volunteer work with similar organisations. Secretarial skills, bookkeeping or accountancy qualifications, entrepreneurial skills adaptable to fund-raising, and communication skills are all valued. Although some posts, at the director or national fund-raising organiser level, attract very good salaries and conditions of service, there are other posts which are part-time or temporary or paid at at a modest level, and these may suit the married woman or the newly-retired.

Here are a few typical examples to illustrate the wide range of work.
A national charity sought a full-time member of staff with special responsibility to its project committee. The ideal candidate would have concern for the elderly, experience with volunteers, enthusiasm and energy, and a good knowledge of the locality. Local authority pay scale was offered. The post was advertised in the local evening paper.

Charity working with probation service. Graduate as assistant organiser — to take a special interest in recruitment, training and deployment of volunteers. Candidates should be lively and energetic.

(A good example of the sort of job that is difficult to classify!) Administrator (initially for six months) for team running funded training project (work experience and ESL) for 16-19 year-olds. Would make some contribution to the training programme itself. Typing essential. Experience in industry and community work an advantage. They wanted details of candidates' education, employment and voluntary work.
Examples of work with two different children's charities.
A personal assistant to the director. Shorthand and typing were essential, and applicants were expected to have 'good intellectual ability and personality, and interest in social work, especially for children'. It was presented as a good chance to familiarize oneself with the administration of the charity.

Part-time, average 15 hours a week during term-time. Must be car-owner. Mileage/expenses and hourly rate of pay by mutual agreement. Although previous experience was not essential, applicants had to be confident they could 'address an audience of children and motivate them to action'.

Incidentally, Help the Aged regularly recruits fund-raisers who visit schools with the twin aims of raising money *and* children's awareness of the importance of the elderly in the community. These are full-time posts, though actual hours are flexible. Training is given and there are some promotion prospects.

Some teachers may take up posts in museums, perhaps working with a school museum service or taking a responsibility for the educational services offered by the museum to children and adults alike. The Museums Association publishes an information sheet on careers in this field, and the monthly periodical *Museums Bulletin*, which includes some vacancies. The Association also publishes the *Museums Yearbook*, which contains a directory of UK museums and galleries.

Perhaps a fairly typical example of a well-established educationalist moving into this field would be that of a science teacher who then worked for some years in teacher training. A strong personal interest was science history and he made good use of museums as a resource in working with student teachers and in curriculum development projects. On the basis of this varied experience, he moved to a post at the Science Museum.

A recent advertisement by a city museum and art gallery gave a very full description of the scope of its museum schools department. The staff consisted of a schools organiser, two assistant organisers, and clerical and technical support staff. They were seeking an assistant (natural history) to join the existing historian and geologist. The new assistant schools organiser was to be a graduate with a teaching qualification and 'practical experience in teaching or museum work'. The organisers were encouraged to work for the Museums Association Diploma. The museum was looking for an imaginative interest in natural history, fieldwork and integrated studies. The job would involve training teachers and students, producing resource materials, and organising and developing the natural history collections of the schools loan service.

Occasionally, posts of a similar nature occur in art galleries. For example, the Civil Service sought an education officer for the National Portrait Gallery. The basic qualifications required were a degree and two years' teaching experience. Paid posts with a schools slant in specialist museums or properties of the National Trust tend to be much sought after. The relevant specialist enthusiasm and voluntary work with the appropriate trust are often key factors in getting such a post.

Publishing is a highly competitive profession but teachers (primary and secondary) have managed to break into it via educational publishing — either on the editorial side or as representatives. Publishing is a comparatively small industry in terms of manpower, employing altogether between 18,000 and 19,000 (including the typists and packers!). Educational publishing, the sector for which teaching experience is most relevant, has recently been adversely affected by the falling school population, cuts in library spending, and the effect of the stronger pound on exports. Even so, it can offer the experienced teacher openings in sales, publicity and, to a lesser degree, in editing functions. Salesmen and women — for more women are entering this job — may these days be involved in running seminars, discussing training schemes with advisers, as well as visiting schools. English as a foreign language is a growth area in textbooks for overseas governments or at chain language-schools' level. The teacher who entered 'hard selling' could expect, if successful, to move into the management side in due course.

Advertisements for both sales and editing functions appear from time to time in *The Bookseller* and national and evening papers. Many publishers, however, never advertise since they receive enough speculative applications. Although many of the graduates who go into publishing are arts graduates, you should not assume that this is a profession just for graduates or only for those who studied the humanities and arts. Languages or a scientific background are extremely useful assets. You need to be a good communicator, and since publishing is an industry, a commercial sense is important.

One publisher told me, 'One of my best members of the sales staff had a variety of temporary teaching posts and a year as a minicab driver'. The variety of his teaching experience and excellent driving are great assets in his new career!

Opportunities also occur in related fields such as preparing resource materials in educational research projects or working in the educational services of radio and television, educational drama and even arts administration. All these jobs, of course, need qualities other than 'five-years-before-the-blackboard' — successful candidates will be able to show some evidence of their interest in the new fields, and probably of related voluntary, freelance or occasional work in it too.

Educational theatre has developed rapidly over the last decade and there is now a variety of schemes, ranging from theatre workshops for children to travelling groups of performers who visit schools. Teachers who move into educational drama as a career are always those with not only enthusiasm for the theatre, but considerable practical involvement. Occasionally, posts appropriate for teachers occur in the educational press or periodicals such as *Community Care*. Theatre vacancies generally, including those with an educational slant, occur in *The Stage*. *Contacts*, a directory of theatrical businesses and services, includes lists of the fringe theatres and educational theatre groups.

Some teachers may move into this field after following a practical postgraduate course, for instance in stage management. Again, appropriate experience would be looked for.

Broadcasting is as competitive a field to enter as the theatre, but both the BBC and ITV have extensive educational services, and many of their staff in this area have had teaching experience. In fact, when I took part in an item on alternative careers for teachers for a Granada television programme, I discovered that three of the four staff with whom I had contact — a researcher, director and the producer — had all trained as teachers!

If you hope to move into this popular career you will almost certainly have some kind of experience of broadcasting, perhaps through involvement in making video programmes with pupils or fellow-teachers, through work on local radio or even hospital radio.

The broadcasting authorities do advertise from time to time, in the national press and in periodicals such as *The Listener*. Where specific educational expertise is sought, the educational press may also be used.

'Arts administration' is a term covering a wide range of jobs — everything from being a secretary or receptionist in a commercial art gallery to being a concert tour organiser, from working in a theatre box office to managing a regional arts centre. Teachers with a creative background and practical experience of organising arts events may find this an attractive field. Skills such as bookkeeping and typing are often very valuable, especially at the lower end of the scale of jobs, and typing remains useful for any arts administrator.

Posts may be advertised in the national press — especially *The Guardian*, and to a lesser extent *The Times* and *The Observer*, in *The Stage*, and *Musical Times*. *Time Out* and *City Limits* and similar publications also carry vacancies. *Opportunities* has local government posts in the field. The Arts Council produces a vacancy bulletin called *Arts Administration* which includes posts notified direct and advertisements culled from magazines and newspapers.

One of the simplest ways of getting an armchair view of the scope of the work is to study this vacancy list over a period of a few months. It will become clear what qualities and skills are sought. A background of some experience in accountancy or commercial administration or leisure and recreation is clearly useful, but there are also posts where a teaching background allied to appropriate practical experience would be most relevant. The sort of appropriate experience would be with local festivals or choirs, art exhibitions, etc. Voluntary as well as paid experience is valuable.

Three posts which I have seen advertised whilst revising this book will illustrate these points. A major national theatre company was looking for an education administrator to maintain and develop its relationships with students and teachers and the whole range of educational institutions. Among the varied duties were organising lecture programmes and workshops, preparing background material for students of all ages, and administering the Summer school which the theatre runs. It sought someone who had a 'well-developed' career as a practitioner in theatre or education (preferably both!). Personal qualities asked for were typical of arts administration advertisements, viz. energy and enthusiasm and the ability to achieve much from 'no resources'!

A community college offered a scale four post as 'head of expressive art'. This was a joint teaching and youth and community post. The duties involved being head of a department incorporating music, drama and dance within a school, administration in connection with the arts centre role of the institution, and development of arts activities within the community. Experience outside school teaching would be an important asset and they saw a knowledge of Caribbean and Asian music as 'helpful'.

The final example is of an educational trust which organised, as part of its programme of training for young people, creative workshops. It advertised for two tutors qualified in drama, art or broadcasting. They needed practical experience and the ability to 'establish constructive relationships' with young people.

The Arts Council bi-monthly *Bulletin* includes details of all short courses for administrators. The City University runs a one-year postgraduate Diploma Course in Arts Administration. Send a self-addressed sticky label or s.a.e. for details if interested.

Self-Employment
It would be presumptuous to suggest that in the space availble to me I can do more than touch upon this area of work, yet many teachers do in fact become self-employed, and not just as private music teachers, coaching for examinations or offering lessons in

foreign languages, though this may be suitable for some. Teachers with appropriate qualifications or specialised skills have become craftsmen or women, or set up small businesses.

If you are considering this strategy, you will probably be aware of the advantages — the freedom and the scope that self-employment offers. It is also important to consider the disadvantages; the lack of security, of a fixed income, the sense of isolation, of having total responsibility in one sense — the buck stops at you and nothing happens unless you make it happen — yet being at the mercy of external factors such as a fluctuating market demand or creditors.

Many small businesses are started each year and many fail. Under-capitalisation, a naive inability to distinguish between net profit and gross income, and a failure to keep proper business accounts of income and expenditure (resulting perhaps in a crippling tax assessment) are all common reasons for failure. As a general rule, it is unwise to enter into full-time self-employment in a field of which you have no commercial experience, unless you can afford to make expensive mistakes. Many advisers would recommend you to make your early mistakes at someone else's expense - as a part-time shop assistant, or working as an employee in a restaurant or hotel, for instance, before sinking your savings in a shop or restaurant on the basis of your flair for fashion or your wife's cordon bleu cooking. There are many sources of advice and help which cost little or nothing and which you should use before launching into self-employment. Reading case histories of the successes and failures of others may be a good introduction to the possible pitfalls. Rosemary Pettit's book *Occupation: Self-Employed* is readable and practical. A book such as *Buying A Shop* by A. St J. Price deals with a specific aspect of self-employment. The ramifications of legal requirements in respect of national insurance contributions, declaration of income to the Inland Revenue and VAT (where applicable), etc. is covered in other books such as *Working for Yourself*. Details are in the bibliography.

Organisations such as the National Federation of Self-Employed in Small Businesses, and the Council for Small Industries in Rural Areas (CoSIRA) produce helpful literature and will give advice. CoSIRA also produces a directory of craft workshops (price £1.25 plus p.& p. charge) which includes retail shops selling craft products, as well as the workshops themselves. In Scotland, the SDA, Small Business Division provides details of both rural and urban craft premises. This may provide useful contacts for those with craft products for which they seek an outlet. The Crafts Council runs schemes to help craftsmen, including one for skills and experience training in the workshop of a master craftsman, and a new craftsman grant for those just setting up in premises of their own. 'Crafts' is a broad term and CoSIRA's directory, for instance, includes boats and canal ware, canework, furniture, musical instruments, saddlery, vehicles and candles, to mention just a few categories, as well as the more obvious jewellery and pottery.

The Small Firms Service of the Department of Industry is an information and counselling service for managers of small businesses. It also provides an advisory service for people thinking of starting their own businesses. It has a network of regional advisers. You can contact it via Freefone 2444.

A number of business schools run short courses on setting up a business, self-employment, etc., so it may be worth contacting the ones in your area to see what is on offer. Tourist Boards can be helpful about enterprises such as guest houses.

Finally, don't forget your friendly bank manager, and at the appropriate point, a solicitor and accountant.

Useful Addresses

Help the Aged
32 Dover Street, London W1A 2AP.

City University, Centre for Arts
Northampton Square, London EC1V 0HB.

National Federation of Self-Employed in Small Businesses
32 St Anne's Road West, St Anne's on Sea, Lancs FY8 1NY.

CoSIRA
141 Castle Street, Salisbury, Wiltshire SP1 3TP.

Scottish Development Agency, Crafts Division
102 Telford Road, Edinburgh EH4 2NG.

Arts Council of Great Britain
105 Picadilly, London W1V 0AU.
(Produces vacancy bulletin 'Arts Administration'.)

Scottish Arts Council
19 Charlotte Square, Edinburgh EH2 4DF.

British Association of Art Therapists
13c Northwood Road, London N6 5TL.

British Association of Drama Therapy
72 Hillmorton Road, Rugby, Warwickshire.
(Has list of mainly short courses, and produces a journal.)

British Association for Counselling
1a Little Church Street, Rugby, Warwickshire CV21 3AP.

British Society for Music Therapy
48 Lanchester Road, London N6 4TA.

Crafts Council
12 Waterloo Place, London SW1Y 4AU.

Scottish Crafts Centre
Acheson House, 140 Canongate, Edinburgh EH8 8DD.

Crafts and Design Dept; Welsh Arts Council
Oriel, 53 Charles Street, Cardiff CF1 3NX.

Careers Service Training Council of the Local Government Training Board
4th Floor, Arndale House, The Arndale Centre, Luton LU1 2TS.

Education and Training Division, The Health Education Council
78 New Oxford Street, London WC1A 1AH.

Scottish Health Education Group
Woodburn House, Canaan Lane, Edinburgh EH10 4SZ.

Guild of Health Education Officers
55 Lower Lickill Road, Stourport-on-Severn, Worcestershire.
Secretary: Mr R.J. Belding.

College of Teachers of the Blind
Lickey Grange School, Old Birmingham Road, Bromsgrove, Worcestershire.
Contact: Mr D.W.F. Folley, BA.
(for details of diploma for teachers of the blind)

Sesame
George Bell House, Bishop's Hall, 8 Ayres Street, London SE1 1ES.
(drama therapy)

Society of Professional Arts Administrators
Flat 5, 86 Worple Road, London SW19.

Museums Association
34 Bloomsbury Way, London WC1A 2SF.

SELL YOURSELF

This section deals with the crucial matter of marketing your talents and experience to potential employers. A great deal of sound advice is available in general books dealing with application and interview techniques, and so the aim here has been to direct attention to aspects of the question which I know from experience are specifically relevant to teachers.

This is a fairly short section, short and I hope very much to the point, as its subject matter 'applications' ought to be.

Your job-search will include vacancy lists from your careers service and/or PER, jobs at the local Jobcentre, possibly ones available through local private employment agencies or recruitment consultancies.

Many jobs, of course, are advertised in the national or local press or specialised journals. *Sources of Vacancies* will give you further information on these sources. But it is obvious that simply because they *are* so readily available to such a wide public, advertised jobs attract large numbers of applications, sometimes in overwhelming proportions. For this reason, and perhaps particularly if you have special experience to offer, it is always a good policy to try to sound out jobs *before* they are advertised, thus giving yourself a head start. In commercial and industrial organisations it is certainly not uncommon for good speculative applications, offering a specific and relevant expertise, to result in a post being created for someone. Vacancies, and their precise duties, are, after all, not fixed, but flexible. At the other end of the spectrum, you may discover nothing more than that there is a possibility of a vacancy in the offing and where it will be advertised. But even this gives you time to research the organisation and gain useful background information, well ahead of the likely opposition. It is as much for this reason, as because of any 'old boys' network, that so often people with contacts (whether relatives, experience of temporary work there, or connections by way of business) with an organisation, are the ones who get the jobs. They already know how to slant their applications so as to appeal to the organisation, and can approach any interview with the security of understanding and presumably being in sympathy with the aims and ethos of the organisation. So speculative applications *are* worth making.

Many small firms may have a vacancy for someone like you, but because their graduate intake is very small, perhaps only one annually, they do not bother to advertise in the directories. Such firms are worth approaching 'cold'.

Making an approach cold to an employer, if it has to have any chance of success, means you need a clear idea of what you can offer and know enough about the business to see where you might fit in. The trade and financial press may be a useful source. Large directories such as *Kompass*, available in large public libraries, are also helpful. With the bigger graduate recruiters, information is much more accessible. Books such as *Which Company?* will give you basic information, and many firms produce recruitment literature, available in the information room of career advisory services in HE institutions. The standard of much of the literature is high; at its best, it gives factual information on the business and structure of the company; the career areas at the graduate level; and something of the character and flavour of the organisation. At the very least, the style of the literature tells you a good deal about the sort of image the company wants to present to the world. Your institution probably also has access to *ROGET*, which includes background information on some of the smaller graduate recruiters.

Alongside your review of actual vacancies, you should, of course, be doing some reading about particular careers and the nature of the work involved.

The range of possible careers is so wide that it is worthwhile making a systematic reappraisal.

You need to have a realistic self-knowledge which includes awareness of:
— your talents and abilities and limitations
— the value of your past experience
— your personal values and attitudes
You also need a realistic job-knowledge which includes awareness of:
— qualities and training needed
— the demands of the job
— the hidden demands (the life-style imposed)
— the incidence of vacancies, and promotion patterns.
The amount of help you will need on all this varies. Some people have very clear ideas about themselves and their needs because one or two aspects of work are of overwhelming importance to them. Others are much less certain. But even people who know exactly what they want may be unaware of crucial aspects of jobs that attract or repel them. If you 'couldn't bear to be cooped up in an office' and describe your main satisfaction as 'helping people', you may find all the report writing and office work

attached to social work both surprising *and* frustrating. Equally, you might dismiss accountancy out of hand because you have confused it with bookkeeping. Your survey of alternative careers should enable you to recognise the snags, but not overlook potential openings out of ignorance.

Personal Checklist

This is not intended as a self-assessment exercise, though it's obviously closely related. It is meant as a reminder of the substantial evidence you can offer in support of your claim that you have skills, abilities and qualities that employers are seeking.

The first part reminds you of the particular crucial qualities and aptitudes you are claiming. The second part gives you space to list all the relevant things you have achieved, knowledge or experience you have acquired, talents you are lucky enough to possess. Of course, you don't tell every potential employer everything — but a checklist of this sort will help you to ensure that, when you make applications, you do not omit some crucial factor which is relevant to a particular job. Equally important, it should help you group your bits of evidence together in a coherent way for the letter element on an application form or for a covering letter to accompany a curriculum vitae (cv).

The examples given in the third column, part b, could not possibly be exhaustive. They are meant as suggestions.

a) Assess yourself in relation to important qualities and strengths:

	GOOD	AVERAGE	LITTLE
Verbal ability...............			
Numeracy....................			
Analytical ability...........			
Creativity...................			
Persuasive skills............			
Others important to you			
....			
....			
....			

b) *Evidence of Skills, Abilities, Qualities, Achievements*
In some areas the level of proficiency can be measured by success in an exam; in others by public acclaim (e.g. in competitive sports, getting public engagements as a musician): in others still, by experience you have enjoyed or survived. *Older people will cull much of their evidence from previous paid employment.* Although this is scarcely mentioned in the examples below to avoid continual repetition, it is obvious and vital. Don't forget it!
Specific Skills
   Languages? (level of fluency as well as exams) Secretarial? Other? Driving Licence?

Talents — (specifically useful in teaching and relevant in other fields)
   Art? Music? Sport? Dramatic ability? (Course taken; exams — highest achieved; teams played for; competitions entered/won; public performances; exhibitions; work published; include college activities or local societies if you didn't make the Olympics or the Royal Academy.)

a) Working with People

Evidence through courses and especially voluntary or paid experience, e.g. adult literacy; helping the handicapped; running a society; working as a sales assistant or in a factory.

Experience with Children

Guiding/Scouting, Sunday School teaching. Taking groups camping; running an adventure playground in the vacation. Fieldwork in a course on slow-learning child; working in a holiday home for children.

Personal Qualities

Organisational ability (committee work for a society; managing domestic life; a degree). Enterprise (running a disco; trekking to remote jungles or mountains; setting up something new; selling anything legal). Leadership (President of SU or chairman of local environmental action group or whatever).

Team work (group projects; committee work; running almost anything from a group base).

Communication Skills

e.g. good at debating; at arguing; presenting written documents in support of a proposal; explaining concepts in simple terms, e.g. to children, ability to communicate through visual means — diagrams etc.

Numeracy

If you are good at figures you probably know it. But others often forget the evidence they have, e.g. 'O' level maths; statistics element in geography or education or any other course.

Problem Solving/Analytical Skills

Finding solutions to practical and organisational problems in following your course; ditto in previous work experience; problem-solving projects within the course.

Commercial Attitudes

Work experience where selling or profit element important; running a function that had to make a profit; working through and enjoying business games, even 'not thinking profit is a dirty word'.

Computer Literacy

Having used computers in one's work; having taken a computer course.

WHAT TEACHERS DID

This section surveys the occupations which we know the newly-qualified teacher has taken up.

The range of careers that teachers have gone into is very wide indeed. Even within one institution the strategies newly-qualified teachers use in beginning or developing their careers are very varied. This is what some of the leavers, who over the last few years have not gone into schools, have done. They all come from the same institution.

Social work assistant with intention of taking CQSW qualification eventually.
Returned to previous occupation as a sugar technologist in a research laboratory (mature student).
Assistant in France.
Short spell as a supply teacher followed by part-time teaching at a sports centre.
Sponsored by Pitmans Secretarial College to take one-year course as teacher of secretarial skills.
After discussions with local careers officer, applied for and obtained permanent position with an insurance company.
Volunteer with VSO.
Undertook nursing training.
Area sales manager, educational publishing house.
Grocery buyer for large retail grocery chain.

Undertook secretarial course.
Media resources officer.
Resident child care officer in children's home.
Civil Service (executive officer, Home Office).
Computer programmer.
Clerical officer, Ministry of Defence.
Sales assistant, then management trainee, retail chain.
Assistant artistic director (for an exhibition).
Nanny (Canada).
Actress, travelling theatre company.
Technician, civic theatre.
Documentalist/librarian, university library.
TEFL, Athens.
Production manager, industrial company.
Translation/secretarial work (through an agency).
Ledger clerk, construction company.
Retail management trainee.
Milk samples analyst.
Housemistress, boarding school.
Leisure officer, theme park.
Reader/braillist language specialist.
Actuary.
Police constable.

The broader national picture is similarly varied. A few years ago, when teaching as a profession lost the job security it had enjoyed since the post-war years, 25 colleges of higher education supplied data, compiled by Margaret Fenwick and Ned Binks, on the destinations of their qualified teachers who did not go into teaching.

Some 50 plus occupations were represented in the list of permanent employment and there were others for which the new teachers were short-listed. Many of these teachers held only a certificate, and not a degree. Here are some of their careers:
Accountancy
Acting
Airline stewardess
Army Education Corps.
Banking
Building society work
Careers officer
Church of England — licensed worker
Civil Service — Executive Officer
Computer work
Customs liaison officer
Dispensing optician — trainee
Draughtsman — trainee
Enamelling
Finance company — management trainee
Grocery buyer — trainee
Health service administration — trainee
Housemistress — boarding school
Insurance company (varied posts)

Journalist
Librarian
Laboratory assistant
Nanny/nursery nurse
Nurse trainee
Outdoor pursuits centre — assistant warden
Playleader
Police
Public house management — trainee
Retail management trainee
Royal Air Force
Safety officer
School photographer's assistant
Self-employed
Social work (resident and non-resident)
Stockbroking — trainee
Youth work

Temporary posts ranged from development officer with a national charity to betting shop manager; stable girl to traffic census enumerator; cinema usherette to work on Teachers Advisory Council on Alcohol and Drug Education.

In 1978, 28 colleges of higher education participated in a survey of leavers' first destinations. This was run under the auspices of the Association of Career Advisers in Colleges of Higher Education (ACACHE) and organised by Dr John Stocks. I am grateful for permission to quote these statistics.
— Of the 3336 certified teachers in the survey, 142 had taken up permanent alternative employment by the end of October of that year.
— Of the 3390 BEd (Ord and Hons) graduates, 164 had taken up such employment.
— Between 7% and 12% of the different categories (PGCE, BEd, CertEd) went into alternative employment (including temporary).
Permanent and temporary employment categories were lumped together in the table showing types of non-teaching posts entered.
— By far the majority went into (1) secretarial/clerical; (2) social welfare; (3) sales and buying; (4)administrative/management categories of work.
By 1981, the ACACHE survey had become an annual exercise covering an estimated 90% of students successfully completing courses in 51 institutions. This represents the output of 83% of the institutions in membership of the Standing Conference of Principals and Directors of Colleges and Institutes of Higher Education.

By now, many of the colleges have much reduced teacher training target numbers and have developed other professional courses and other degree courses. Of the total of qualified teachers whose destinations are known (6269), 80.6% are known to have been employed at the date of survey. 13.5% were unemployed, and the others were either not available, following further courses, or were overseas students returning home.

Out of the 4236 in employment, 345 teachers went into permanent employment other than teaching or lecturing in the UK. This includes 115 PGCE leavers, 189 BEds, 37 CertEds and 4 leavers from specialist courses. Additionally, the survey noted 107 known to be working abroad, and a further 74 who have taken up temporary work abroad. The classification of types of work is the same as that followed by other sectors of higher education for their graduates. The largest group went into work classified as 'Social,

Medical and Security', and substantial groups went into 'Administration/Operational Management' and 'Buying, Marketing, Selling'. 23 teachers managed to get jobs defined as 'Creative and Entertainment' despite the competition in this field of work.

From time to time, I meet criticism of this steady move of a significant minority of newly-trained teachers into jobs other than teaching. 'What a waste of the expensive training!' is the cry. But I think such criticism is ill-founded. Those who do not go into schools are spread across the different employer categories. In 1981, for instance, 3.4% went into public service, 2.3% into industry or commerce and the remainder (2.3%) into a range of other organisations. Some of these teachers will make considerable headway in their new professions and eventually be in positions of some influence within their own sphere. But they will still be people who have actually taught in schools (on teaching practice) and learnt a great deal about the educational system and its aims and philosophy. By far the majority of them, even though they have chosen to do something else, have a sympathy for and understanding of the tasks demanded of teachers — and to have influential staff in industry, commerce and the public services, who actually know something about schools, cannot be a bad thing for the teaching profession! Education needs all the destroyers of myths and promoters of balanced views it can get!

USEFUL REFERENCE BOOKS

Most of the books listed below should be available through libraries, but many are the sort you would want to buy and cost no more than a pound or two. Obviously you wouldn't buy them all unless you are setting up an adult advisory centre! I have tried to indicate the content and intended audience of each book and what seem to me its main strengths. Books that may be too expensive for most people to consider purchasing, but which you should find in a reference library are indicated by †. Recruitment directories which are also expensive to purchase but which are obtainable free by final year undergraduates through their institution's careers advisory service are indicated by ‡.

†*Annual Careers Guide* — Careers and Occupational Information Centre (COIC) of the Manpower Services Commission.
Covers professions, public services, commerce and industry in all the areas of work that offer 'careers' as opposed to 'jobs' — beginning with account executive and ending with zoology, via such possibilities as artificer, freight forwarder and neurophysiology technician. The index alone is worth consulting if you are uninspired.

Back to Work — Cathy Moulder and Pat Sheldon, Kogan Page, 1979.
Directed at potential women 'returners'. Discusses the pros. and cons. of returning to work and gives very brief details of some 70 jobs which may be of interest.

Careers A to Z — Ruth Lancashire and Roger Holdsworth, Hobsons Press, 1976.
Well deserves its reputation as one of the most sound general guides for adults considering a change of career.

†*Careers Encyclopedia* — ed. Audrey Segal, Cassell, 10th edition.
Classified, not alphabetically as most careers guides are, but according to 'fields' of work. For example, 'Professional, Scientific and Social Services' includes teaching and translating, whilst 'Creative, Communicative, Cultural and Entertainment' includes librarianship and professional sport. It is an interesting attempt at classification which may stimulate some creative thinking about possible careers. A useful section on opportunities abroad.

Coping with Interviews Martin Higham, New Opportunity Press, 1982.
Words of wisdom from a highly experienced graduate recruiter with a mind and style of his own. Particularly directed at the recent graduate, with more emphasis on commerce and industry than on the social and welfare jobs but much of the advice is applicable more generally.

†*Directory of Further Education* — Careers Research and Advisory Centre (CRAC) (annual).
Useful directory for those considering further training. Should be available in libraries.

Directory of Independent Training and Tutorial Organisations Elizabeth Summerson and Maureen Davis, Careers Consultants, 1981.
Just what its title suggests. A very useful guide to a wide variety of vocational courses offered by the private sector — from lace-making to estate management, commercial diving to modelling. Sensible advice about financing courses and about accreditation.

The Directory of Jobs and Careers Abroad — ed. Philip Dodd, Vacation Work, 5th edition. 1982.
General advice on finding work abroad, immigration requirements, etc. Chapters on opportunities for specific professions including teachers. Entries on individual countries giving background information and useful addresses for those seeking work there. Emphasis on Europe and the West but includes a section on the Middle East and North Africa and Japan.

‡*Directory of Opportunities for Graduates* — Haymarket (annual).
Carries a large number of recruiters' advertisements some of which give quite a lot of information (not, of course, unbiased!!) about the organisation.

Dismissal, Redundancy and Job-hunting — ed. Edith Rudinger, Consumers' Association.
Factual guide covering legal aspects of dismissal and redundancy, unemployment benefit, etc. But also has a section on coping with interviews.

A Directory of Voluntary Counselling and Allied Services — British Association for Counselling, 1978.
Details of between 500 and 600 voluntary counselling services listed on a regional basis. May be a useful guide to those seeking involvement in counselling on a voluntary basis. Also indicates if agency employs paid staff.

Equal Opportunities — Ruth Miller, Penguin.
The up-dated version of that useful stand-by *Careers for Girls*. Although it includes a

large number of careers which appeal to men, its origins suggest it might be particularly helpful to women wanting a realistic assessment of opportunities for them.

Finding Another Top Job — Bill Lubbock, IPM, 1975.
Directed at redundant senior executives in industry and commerce. The author adopts an unorthodox stand-point, arguing that such people should not concentrate on replying to advertisements, but instead should seek out a job *before* the firm advertises.

There are, therefore, some very interesting sections on doing research on likely companies and drafting speculative letters in order to secure an interview. Thought-provoking; likely to be useful mainly to older graduates with previous experience.

Getting the Job You Want — Howard Dowding and Sheila Boyce, Ward Lock, 1979.
General advice to the job-hunter including detailed sections on filling in application forms and preparing for interviews. Includes a number of interesting sample letters both 'good' and 'poor' and an analysis of them. Not all authorities would agree with its dicta on what to omit.

Getting the Right Job — Chris Parsons and Angela Neustatter, Pan Books, 1979.
General advice on both planning a career and getting a job. Directed at both school and college leavers. Inevitably individual topics dealt with briefly, but valuable for its interesting personal case histories.

The Good Job Guide — New Opportunity Press, 1981.
Includes a directory of employers (many of whom are included in the graduate recruitment directories). There is also a very useful list of recruitment consultants and private employment agencies. General articles on making applications etc.

‡*Graduate Employment and Training* — Careers Research and Advisory Centre (CRAC) (annual).
Useful for graduates but also for other students with higher education qualifications. There are some helpful articles on personal interests, abilities and values, and occupations; and valuable sections on the degree subjects from which particular employers recruit, and graduate exemptions from professional qualifications.

‡*Graduate Opportunities* — New Opportunity Press (annual).
Directory of graduate employment opportunities, similar to DOG and GET.

‡*Graduate Studies* — Careers Research and Advisory Centre (CRAC) (annual)
A standard guide to postgraduate courses of study from vocational courses to areas of study for doctoral research.

A Guide to Voluntary Work Opportunities — National Youth Bureau 1980 (with amendment list 1981).
Details of organisations welcoming volunteers.

‡*Handbook of Recruitment Services* — compiled with assistance of Federation of Personnel Services.

How to be Interviewed — D. Mackenzie Davey, P. McDonnell, BIM Foundation, 1980.
Authors are management consultants who are involved in training interviewers. So although this is a brief, rather jokey guide, it's worth knowing what the 'opposition' thinks.

How to Cope with Redundancy — Norman H. Page, Mantec Publications, 1975.
Directed at redundant commercial and industrial professional staff. The chapters on compiling a personal inventory, writing letters of application, etc. are, however, of general applicability, especially for the older job-seeker.

How to Get a Job — Marjorie Harris, Institute of Personnel Management, Central House, Upper Woburn Place, London WC1H 0HX, 1979.
A useful brief basic guide to this all-important question.

The International Directory of Voluntary Work — R. Brown and D. Woodworth, Vacation Work, 1979.
Details of volunteer (including 'paid' volunteer) opportunities, both long-term and short-term and part-time, residential and non-residential, in Europe and elsewhere. There are sections on work with children, in educational schemes, and relating to prison and probation work.

Job Sharing: A Guide for Employers — New Ways to Work, 1981

Job Sharing: A Guide for Employees — New Ways to Work, 1982.
A lively practical booklet with advice on finding a job-sharing partner and examples of success to quote or inspire.

Job-Sharing: improving the quality and availability of part-time work — Equal Opportunities Commission, 1981.
An examination of the practical implications of this arrangement.

†*Kompass (UK)*.
Regional directories of industrial companies. Should be available in large public commercial libraries.

Occupation Self-Employed — Rosemary Pettit, Wilwood House Ltd., 1981.
The earlier edition gave suggestions for self-employment from selling antiques to bee keeping; teaching English as a foreign language to running a pub. The original case histories have been followed up and are both readable and informative. Includes those who had to return to employment as well as those whose businesses prospered.

A Practical Guide to Making Money at Home — Olga Franklin, Macdonald and Co., 1981.
Basically a stimulating collection of possibilities for self-employment.

Second Chances 1983 — Andrew Pates and Martin Good, Great Ouse Press.
Fills a big gap in educational information. Describes the wide range of education and training opportunities for adults. A lively and lucid guide through a bewildering maze of provision. Perhaps of particular interest to teachers who are considering retraining (e.g. through TOPS) and those who are hoping to teach in FE and want to understand its ramifications. Lots of names and addresses.

Self Employment Factbook — Nigel Prentis, Great Ouse Press, 1983.
An excellent starting point for people thinking of becoming self-employed. Explains tax, national insurance, bookkeeping, VAT, when to use professional advisers and much more in a simple, straightforward way.

Summer Jobs Abroad — Vacation Work, 9 Park End St., Oxford (annual).
Details of temporary posts covering range of temporary jobs, including work in children's holiday centres, camps, etc, hotel work, teaching English as a foreign language.

Summer Jobs in Britain (annual).
Similar publication, same publisher.

TES Guide to Careers in Education — ed. Tony Howarth, Nelson, 1977.
A useful detailed guide to a wide range of educational careers, with descriptive short essays, addresses, bibliographies, etc.

Temporary Occupations and Employment — ed. Joan Hills, Independent Schools Careers Organisation, 12a/18a Princess Way, Camberley, Surrey GU15 3SP.
Directed at the school-leaver, but contains many useful addresses and notes on various schemes and agencies.

Voluntary Organisations Bedford Square Press, 1982.
Comprehensive directory of all kinds of voluntary bodies.

Volunteer Bureaux Directory 1981-2. The Volunteer Centre.
Directory of bureaux which recruit and place volunteers. Listed by town, region, etc.

Which Company? - The Daily Telegraph Guide to British Employers Kogan Page Ltd., 1978.
Directed at 'both experienced executive and newly-qualified men' in the industrial and commercial fields. Background information (factual) on 700 of 'Britain's top firms' and a smaller number of fuller (advertisement) features. Useful articles on how to find out about an employer and how to cope with an interviewer. These articles are geared to the needs of the experienced applicant, but they contain some interesting suggestions for the recent graduate too.

Working Holidays — Central Bureau for Educational Visits and Exchanges (annual).
Broader in scope than the title implies, it covers information on teacher exchange and language assistants posts abroad, practical information on visas, passports, insurance, low cost air fares, etc. and information on temporary paid and volunteer engagements both in the UK and abroad.

Working for Yourself Godfrey Golzen, Kogan Paul, 1980.
A major section of the book deals with the business side of things like accounting systems, taxation and cash flow forecasting, but there are many suggestions from DJ work to letting rooms, including a substantial element on running shops and other business premises.

SOURCES OF VACANCIES

The following list gives you some idea of the journals and newspapers which carry advertisements you want to read.

Newspapers

The Daily Telegraph (very broad range indeed — often has unusual and unexpected posts tucked away in its lengthy columns, but many posts need experience)

The Guardian (strong on public appointments and teaching and has a creative/media section once a week)

The Observer (reputation as being good for new graduates)

The Sunday Telegraph (general)

The Sunday Times (general — very wide range)

The Times (general — an interesting selection of secretarial and PA posts)

The Times Educational Supplement (teaching of course!! Also educational administration, counselling, youth work, community work, further education, etc.)

The 'middle-brow' dailies may also offer suitable opportunities. *The Daily Mail* for example carries residential social worker posts and public appointments aimed at 'O' and 'A' level qualifications. Some provincial papers such as *The Manchester Evening*

News, The Yorkshire Post and the *Western Mail* offer a very wide range of posts within their circulation areas. Weekly newspapers of a specialist or denominational character may also offer opportunities. *The Universe* for example offers posts in RC schools. *The Times Higher Educational Supplement* carries posts in FE, youth work, the careers service, etc., also educational administration. *The Times Literary Supplement* is noted for library posts.

Periodicals and Advertising Broadsheets
These are a few examples.
Teaching:
Contact (ILEA)
New Society
The Teacher

Social Work:
New Society
Social Work Today
Community Care

Work with Children
General:
The Lady (assistant matrons, housemistresses, ancillary staff, nannies)
Nursery World (nannies, nursery governesses, nursery nurses and assistants, occasional teaching vacancies in nursery schools and playgroups).

Specialist Interests
Nature
Habitat
Computer Weekly
Museum Bulletin
New Scientist
The Economist
The Listener

Public Service Appointments
Opportunities
The Kind of Jobs They Advertise The range of jobs advertised by newspapers is very wide. It is worth looking through the columns regularly remembering that the uninspiring-sounding 'General', 'Office', 'Secretarial' headings can top some interesting and unusual positions. (But allow for the fact that the advertiser is trying to attract the reader and expect a bit of poetic licence in the job description!) Here are a few examples of jobs advertised in the past twelve months in journals. Some of these posts are intended for people with experience and are included to show where a fairly routine first job, or a particular combination of qualifications and interests, might lead.

Job	Salary	Organisation	Qualifications Etc.	Journal	Placings Etc.
Assistant Housemother	not given	Charitable Home for Mentally Handicapped Children	Over 21, experience in care of children. Willing to take responsibility.	Evening paper	Classified ads.
Assistant Keeper, Extension Services	£5652-£7875 dependent on quals. and exp.	City Industrial Museum	Graduate, preferably teaching qual. and experience, and/or museums diploma.	*The Guardian*	Display
Secretary/ Shorthand typist	state sal. required	Classical Museum Publisher	Able to run small office. Knowledge of bookkeeping. Possibly a music graduate.	*The Guardian*	Semi-display
Community Leisure Officer (play)	£5064-£5526	Borough Council	Duties include: developing resource centre, running holiday play scheme. Must have wide experience in children's play.	*Opportunities*	Classified
Team Leader, Youth Opportunities Programme	£5547-£6009	Borough Council	Ability to teach unemployed school-leavers 'personal relationship skills, life skills and, if possible, car maintenance'.	*Opportunities*	Classified
Conservator, Environment Dept.	£7371-£7875	Local Authority	Degree biology or environmental science. Strong interest conservation. Experience teaching or youth work advantage. Must have current driving licence. Work involves liaison schools and youth clubs.	*Opportunities*	Classified

Job	Salary	Organisation	Qualifications Etc.	Journal	Placings Etc.
Part-time helper to assist physiotherapist	£1.80 to £2.12 per hour	Health Authority	Physically fit, willing to help old and disabled people.	Local paper (weekly)	Semi-display
House-parent/ Therapist	£5628–£7217	School for Children with Special Needs	Caring qualities. Ability to work in team of paramount importance. Especially welcome those with interest in sport, outdoor activities, rural studies, music, technology.	*Community Care*	Display
Instructors (woodwork, horticulture, social education, craft)	£4926–£6696 dep. on quals.	Centre for Mentally Handicapped Adults	Preference given to those with relevant quals. Craft should involve more than usual knitting, macrame'ac, etc.	*Social Work Today*	Display
Research and Information Officer	£4500–£5500	University Students Union	To research student trends and problems. Provide information on students' rights. Experience in higher education or students' unions.	*Times Higher Education Supplement*	Display 'Research Studentships' heading
Teacher on Intermediate Treatment Course	Burnham Scale 2	Children's Charity	Job will involve input in education programme, counselling, court work, group work.	*Community Care*	Display
Regional Executive Officer	£5273–£7247 overtime for evening/ weekend work	Sports Council	Aged — 20s. Prof. qual. in PE and/or recreation. Willing work some evenings and weekends.	*Opportunities*	Classified

Job	Salary	Organisation	Qualifications Etc.	Journal	Placings Etc.
Full-time Worker, Advisory Centre	£6750	Educational Advisory Body	Flexible. Committed. Experience in as many as possible of: education/rights work/clerical/administration/lobbying/organising meetings/magazine production including writing.	The Guardian	'Creative and Media' display
Regional Officer	£5652-£6333	Charity for Disabled	Able to identify needs, liaise statutory and voluntary bodies, educational work with schools and probably fund-raising. Graduate with 'drive and commitment' and current driving licence.	The Guardian	'Creative and Media' display
Resident Warden, Student Nurses' Home	£4230-£5117	Hospital	Comparable experience and sympathetic and caring approach to young people.	Local paper (weekly)	Semi-display
Senior Administrator	not given	Charitable Body	Aged 30-40. 'Mature outlook, amiable disposition, ability to fit in'. Practical experience or knowledge: trust or charity law, educational grants and finance or social security valuable. Experience in solicitor's office could be helpful.	Observer	Semi-display
PA/Secretary to Director, Market Research	c.£6000	International Company	Fast accurate typing. Knowledge German useful.	The Times	Small ads.

Job	Salary	Organisation	Qualifications Etc.	Journal	Placings Etc.
Personal Assistant to Managing Director	£6300, negotiable	Publishing Company (via a recruitment agency)	Good layout important. Interest in English literature. Fast shorthand not essential.	*The Times*	'Crème de la Crème' display
Personal Assistant to President	£8000	American Film Company	Good secretarial and administrative skills. Must be bi-lingual. Some travelling.	*The Times*	'Crème de la Crème' display
Project leader/ Director	£106 per week	Community Arts Project	Teaching qual. in drama, wide experience theatre, youth clubs, community projects, etc. Able to drive and use own vehicle. Must be unemployed.	*The Stage*	Display
Box Office Manager	not given	Theatre	Aged late 20s. Experience of office administration and working with people.	*Time Out*	Small ads.
Medical Representatives (trainees)	not given	Recruitment Agency	22-30 yrs. Life science degree, SRN or training qual.	*Daily Telegraph*	Classified ads. 'Representatives'
Assistant Superintendent (trainee)	not given, 'Good Salary'	Seamen's Mission	Church membership. Willingness to learn about caring for fishing community.	*Daily Telegraph*	Classified ads. 'General'
Assistant to Chief Executive	£7500-£8000	Voluntary Organisation running Homes and Hostels	Aptitude for problem solving, admin. and decision-making. Outgoing personality able to handle crises.	*Daily Telegraph*	Classified ads.

ABBREVIATIONS EXPLAINED

Although my policy is to give in full the title of any organisation the first time it is mentioned, and though many of the initials used subsequently will be familiar to teachers, sixth formers, for example, may find them confusing. I hope the reference to this list will prove a useful way of resolving any possible confusion in the text.

ACACHE	Association of Careers Advisers in Colleges of Higher Education
AGCAS	Association of Graduate Careers Advisory Services
ARELS	Association of Recognised English Language Schools
BA	Bachelor of Arts
BEd	Bachelor of Education
BSc	Bachelor of Science
CAS	Careers Advisory Service
CCETSW	Central Council for Education and Training of Social Workers
COIC	Careers and Occupational Information Centre
CP	Community Programme
CRAC	Careers Research and Advisory Centre
CQSW	Certificate of Qualification in Social Work

CSV	Community Service Volunteers
CV	curriculum vitae (Details of one's education, qualifications, experience, etc. presented in a concise tabulated form for job applications).
DES	Department of Education and Science
DHSS	Department of Health and Social Security
DOG	*Directory of Opportunities for Graduates* (employment opportunities directory)
EFL	English as a foreign language
ESL	English as a second language
FE	Further education
FELCO	Federation of English Language Course Organisations
GCE	General Certificate of Education
GET	*Graduate Employment and Training* (employment opportunities directory)
GO	*Graduate Opportunities* (employment opportunities directory)
HE	Higher education
HMSO	Her Majesty's Stationery Office
IAPS	The Incorporated Association of Preparatory Schools
ISIS	Independent Schools Information Service
LEA	Local Education Authority
MA	Master of Arts
MEd	Master of Education
MSC	Manpower Services Commission
MSc	Master of Science
NATFHE	National Association of Teachers in Further and Higher Education
NPFA	National Playing Fields Association
NTI	New Training Initiative
PE	Physical Education
PER	Professional and Executive Recruitment
PGCE	Postgraduate Certificate in Education
RAEC	Royal Army Education Corps
RAF	Royal Air Force
RSA	Royal Society of Arts
TEFL	Teaching English as a foreign language
TES	*Times Educational Supplement* (weekly educational newspaper)
TOPS	Training Opportunities Programmes
TUC	Trade Union Congress
UCCA	Universities Central Council on Admissions
VSO	Voluntary Services Overseas
YMCA	Young Men's Christian Association
YOP	Youth Opportunities Programme
YTS	Youth Training Scheme

INDEX OF OCCUPATIONS REFERRED TO

95